Russ Alan Prince | **Richard L. Harris**

ADVANCED PLANNING
with the ULTRA-AFFLUENT

A Framework for Professional Advisors

ADVANCED PLANNING WITH THE ULTRA-AFFLUENT

A FRAMEWORK FOR PROFESSIONAL ADVISORS

Institutional Investor NEWSLETTERS

© Russ Alan Prince, 2002

New York editorial and publishing offices:
488 Madison Avenue, 14th floor
New York, New York 10022
(212) 224-3300

ISBN number 1-893339-94-7

FOR JERRY,
JUST LIKE THAT.
RUSS ALAN PRINCE

TO MY TREASURES,
PAULA AND OUR CHILDREN.
RICHARD L. HARRIS

RUSS ALAN PRINCE
www.iihighnetworth.com

Russ Alan Prince, president of the market research and consulting firm Prince & Associates LLC, is a leading expert on the private wealth industry and on advisor-based distribution.

Russ consults for leading financial institutions on strategic and marketing issues. He is called upon to develop strategic marketing plans, for tactical competitive advice, and for guidance on expanding presence through strategic alliances, product development, and executive development.

He provides a variety of coaching and consulting services to financial advisors who target affluent markets. Russ is a seasoned developer of proprietary prospecting and sales and relationship management systems, and he also provides high-end customized practice management programs.

RICHARD L. HARRIS
Richard@bpnmont.com

Richard L. Harris is the managing member of BPN Montaigne LLC, a firm that is devoted to advising the affluent on wealth enhancement, wealth transfer, asset protection, and philanthropic planning.

Richard is a problem solver for the very rich, specializing in creative solutions that take into account their personal desires, concerns, and financial complexities. In conjunction with his advisory board and professional network, he brings together expertise and cutting-edge ideas to craft scenarios that integrate and address the issues at hand.

He provides educational seminars to financial professionals regarding various advanced planning concepts, their uses and applicability. In addition, Richard consults with and supports professionals in situations about which they have concerns and need information or ideas.

Institutional Investor | NEWSLETTERS

This book is brought to you by Institutional Investor Newsletters, the editors of Private Asset Management. Our biweekly issues deliver the high-net-worth strategies, competitive intelligence, and proprietary survey data to money managers, private bankers, family offices, hedge funds, and financial advisors. Readers gain insight into fee structures, new products, and marketing strategies from top investment firms. Private bankers depend on Private Asset Management as the most in-depth and timely source of information for their businesses.

www.iihighnetworth.com

www.iiwealthmanagement.com

TABLE | OF CONTENTS

Part I

PERSPECTIVES ON WEALTH

Part III

AT THE CUTTING EDGE

Part IV

IMPLICATIONS FOR PROFESSIONAL ADVISORS

Part V

APPENDICES

LIST

OF EXHIBITS

Chapter 5

Chapter 6

Chapter 7

Chapter 8

Appendices

PRIVATE ASSET MANAGEMENT, Institutional Investor's flagship newsletter focused on the high-net-worth market, has long been regarded as the thought leader on the affluent markets. Over the years, to address the needs of our readership, we have written books and developed a seminar series to further explore the dynamic changes in this marketplace.

The ultra-affluent represent an exceptionally attractive market for financial as well as other advisors. In examining the preferences and concerns of the readership it became apparent that we needed to move beyond investment management and focus on advanced planning.

What we also learned was that those involved in the private wealth industry agreed that the time to look at this segment was certainly now. They agreed that the ultra-affluent are the strategic high-ground for all those jockeying for a share of the private client universe. They also expressed a very strong interest in those wealth management services few are expert in — advanced planning.

Once the decision was made to look at the ultra-affluent in the context of advanced planning, we approached Russ Alan Prince to research this market and write a book based upon the results. As the leading expert on the private wealth industry, he has written 20 books in the field of private wealth, moderates cutting-edge executive seminars, and he consults with leading financial institutions, professional firms, and elite advisors.

Russ, with the assistance of Richard L. Harris, spearheaded the project, and produced an essential tool for anyone focused on advance planning for the ultra-affluent market.

Richard L. Harris is the managing member of BPN Montaigne LLC, a firm that is devoted to advising the ultra-affluent on wealth enhancement, wealth transfer, asset protection, and philanthropic planning. While Russ provides a strategic perspective, Richard brings extensive in-the-trenches experience to the project.

Any financial institution, law firm, accounting firm or advisor interested in serving this highly profitable and demanding segment of the affluent will greatly benefit from *Advanced Planning With the Ultra-Affluent*.

Nazneen Kanga
Publisher, Institutional Investor Newsletters
November 2001

ABOUT

THIS BOOK

ADVICE, N. THE SMALLEST CURRENT COIN.
Ambrose Bierce

I'M NOT A TEACHER: ONLY A FELLOW TRAVELER
OF WHOM YOU ASKED THE WAY. I POINTED AHEAD —
AHEAD OF MYSELF AS WELL AS YOU.
George Bernard Shaw

The long bull run for the American economy that commenced in 1982 produced astounding wealth and swelled the ranks of American millionaires as never before. The boom also created a parallel surge in the demand for advisory services for the wealthy, particularly among the "ultra-affluent" — those who have a net worth of $25 million or more. Indeed, when the Internet bubble burst in 2000, the damage it inflicted on the portfolios and psyches of wealthy Americans only heightened their belief in the value of professional guidance.

This book takes a very focused view of one segment of the private wealth market for advice: advanced planning for the ultra-affluent. It is not a "how-to" guide explaining the concepts of advanced planning. Indeed, the financial techniques, strategies and products mentioned throughout are current examples. The only prediction we can make about them is that there will be change. It is instead a "what's next" book for successful advanced planners who already have such clients and want to further refine their business models.

Based on extensive research conducted by Prince & Associates, we will zero in on the size and composition of the growing ultra-affluent population, the needs and expectations of its members with regard to advanced planning, and how professional advisors can best satisfy those needs and expectations.

With the maze of financial options and issues confronting the wealthy today, there has never been a greater demand for informed advisors — or a greater opportunity for those professional advisors to extend and improve their relationships with ultra-affluent clients. This book was written to help those advisors take that next step with confidence and insightfulness.

Part I

PERSPECTIVES
ON WEALTH

The ultra-affluent are the rara avis
of private clients, and knowing more
about them — who they are, how
they came to be wealthy, the nature
of their goals and expectations —
will help advanced planners improve
and extend their client relationships.

VARIETIES
OF AFFLUENCE

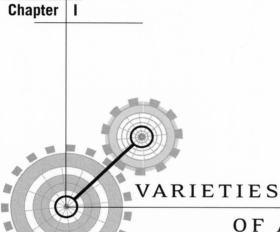

VARIETIES
OF AFFLUENCE

The ranks of the ultra-affluent have never been larger and, with a range of tax issues and financial options to contend with, the ultra-affluent are increasingly dependent on professional advisors to help them clarify and achieve their personal and financial agendas.

WEALTH IS NOT WITHOUT ITS ADVANTAGES AND
THE CASE TO THE CONTRARY, ALTHOUGH IT HAS OFTEN
BEEN MADE, HAS NEVER PROVED PERSUASIVE.

John Kenneth Galbraith

Making money is one of the cardinal American virtues, right up there with freedom of speech and the vote, and seldom before have so many people so fully and successfully exercised their right to wealth as they have at the turn of the 21st century. Forget Renaissance Italy and the Gilded Age; dollar for dollar, there has never been a time or place with as many rich people as America today.

And for Americans, as always, the making and spending of money is a great spectator sport. From the spice traders of the 18th century down through the railroad barons, oilmen, junk-bond traders, and dot.com entrepreneurs, rich Americans have long been the center of media and public attention. It often seems as if the next best thing to being rich is watching the rich spend their money. That is why the market for lists and information about the lifestyles of the super-rich is inexhaustible, and why more people can probably name the richest man in America than the Vice President of the United States. People who have never seen Alex Rodriquez swing a bat or field a grounder nonetheless know that he is "the $250 million-dollar man" — the highest paid athlete in the history of sports.

THE MILLIONAIRE ROLLCALL

The IRS would be hard-pressed to quantify the number of millionaires in America, but most people use the ballpark figure of five million — one out of every 60 citizens. The most staggering jump has come over the last quarter century: In 1975, there were 90,000 American millionaires; today, according to some estimates, there are at least five million (and, by our analysis, many more). In other words, the number of millionaires has at the very least increased more than 55-fold in 25 years. Talk about fulfilling the American dream.

THE WEALTHIEST OF THE WEALTHY

Those are the statistics for garden-variety millionaires, but what of the people in the financial penthouse, the wealthiest of the wealthy? Again, there are no definitive figures to cite. However, the Forbes 400, an informal but highly visible measure of national wealth, is a pretty good snapshot of the super-rich, and it offers some compelling numbers. In 1982, the first year the list was published, the top spot was held by Daniel Keith Ludwig with "above two billion," one of just 13 billionaires on the list, and the cut-off point for making the list was $93 million. The numbers on the most recent list, published in October of 2000, are so much higher that one might conclude that Forbes was comparing different centuries or using another currency such as the lira. Bill Gates is top-dog with $63 billion and the cut-off point has soared to $725 million. The total wealth of the 400 is $1.2 trillion — a new high — and there are 298 billionaires with a formidable median net worth of $3 billion. Finally, Forbes estimates that there are now 4,000 Americans who have more than $100 million.

The increase in wealth can be attributed to the fact that, despite the recent downturn, investments in just about everything — stocks, bonds, land, art — have had outsized returns in the last decade. The Dow Jones Industrial Average, for example, rose 318 percent in the 1990s. Investing has not been the only broker of ultra-affluence, however. There was also invention and those high-profile, t-shirted slackers who made millions on the Internet. Looking ahead, many people have concluded that inheritance will be the leading minter of American millionaires over the next quarter century as the parents of Baby Boomers die and pass on their wealth. And, as our research concludes, the exclusive club of the ultra-affluent will continue to grow apace.

THE BULL MARKET FOR ADVICE

The rich want to stay rich, of course, or better yet, become richer, so they are looking for ways to manage — and grow — their wealth. And, more importantly, from the advanced planner's perspective, they need to make sure it will sustain the lifestyle of current and possibly future generations. But at the same time that wealth has increased, so have the number of options and decisions facing the wealthy. If one looks at the low-end of the ultra-affluent scale, those with a net worth of $25 million, and took the least daring approach, parking all of their wealth in a savings account with a 4 percent annual return — just a step above keeping it in a mattress — it would still produce $1 million a year in interest, assuming no compounding. The vast majority of the ultra-affluent are aiming a lot higher however, wanting to diversify across a wide range of styles and vehicles and to concentrate on wealth enhancement strategies and tactics to maximize tax efficiency. And, time and time again, studies have shown that affluent individuals want help; in fact, the more money they have, the more interested they are in advisors.

AN OVERVIEW

This book was written to address that growing market for advisors, advanced planners in particular, and the expectations that the ultra-affluent have of those advisors. In this section, *Perspectives on Wealth*, we will examine the size of the ultra-affluent segment and the characteristics of its members. In Part II, we will take a closer look at the nature of *Advanced Planning* for the ultra-affluent, and then, in Part III, *At the Cutting Edge*, see how advanced planners create and incorporate the latest innovations into their existing business models. Lastly, in Part IV, *Implications for Professional Advisors*, we will examine the best practices of some of today's top advanced planners who work with this affluent segment.

First off, however, we will size the opportunity by scientifically estimating how many ultra-affluent there are out there and how fast their ranks are growing by developing an analytic model.

OUR METHODOLOGY

For professional advisors, for our purposes, those who provide advanced planning services to the ultra-affluent, the most relevant issue is not the fact of the ultra-affluent market, but its size which, in turn, helps determine the business opportunity. To that end, Prince & Associates developed an analytical model to calculate the size of the affluent market.

Sizing the affluent universe, as we have already inferred, is daunting. There is no master list and many of the ultra-affluent understandably prefer anonymity to ward off bothersome solicitations and protect their privacy. As a result, we turned to analytic modeling to size and scope the private wealth market. The model incorporated data from 133 different sources such as think tanks, financial institutions, industry consultants, academicians, and governmental organizations. The sources included Merrill Lynch, the Spectrem Group, New York University, the Lazard Trust, the Soloton Society, the World Bank, Cornell University, and the International Association for Research in Income and Wealth. (For a detailed explanation of our model and methodology, please refer to **Appendix 1: Analytic Modeling** on page 173.)

LEVELS OF AFFLUENCE

The analytic model allowed us to create a number of possible estimates. In each case, there is a best estimate, a low-end estimate, and a high-end estimate. The accuracy of these various estimates is determined by sensitivity analysis. Prior to examining the estimates in detail, let's delineate the levels within the affluent class of millionaires (Exhibit 1.1).

Exhibit 1.1

VARIETIES OF AFFLUENCE

LEVEL	WEALTH RANGE
Low-End Affluent	$1M to $5M
Affluent	$5M to $25M
Supra-Affluent	$25M to $150M
Mega-Affluent	$150M to $500M
Maxi-Affluent	$500M+

The low-end affluent have a net-worth of $1 million to $5 million and, for the most part, the members of these familial units do not consider themselves wealthy — they are often representative of the group known as "middle class millionaires." Furthermore, a relatively small proportion of their wealth is liquid. The affluent control from $5 million to $25 million in assets. According to most advisors, we are now starting to talk about the rich. The next three levels, who have a minimum of $25 million, comprise the ultra-affluent.

As part of sizing the affluent market we were able to calculate how many familial units were in each of these levels of affluence and our best estimate is that there are more than 17 million familial units worldwide who are millionaires (Exhibit 1.2). As might be expected, the vast majority are among the low-end affluent, but our best estimate of the ultra-affluent population is 68,570. And, as a group, the ultra-affluent controls nearly $12 trillion in assets (Exhibit 1.3). Keeping in mind that most of these people will have a team of advisors to address their many financial needs, that number represents a sizable market opportunity.

Exhibit 1.2

THE AFFLUENT POPULATION

LEVEL	LOW-END ESTIMATE	BEST ESTIMATE	HIGH-END ESTIMATE
Low-End Affluent	15,488,000	16,712,000	19,824,000
Affluent	442,680	531,610	645,510
Supra-Affluent	49,220	58,990	62,380
Mega-Affluent	5,670	7,640	8,691
Maxi-Affluent	1,170	1,940	2,580
Total	15,986,740	17,312,180	20,543,161
Ultra-Affluent*	**56,060**	**68,570**	**73,651**

* Includes the Supra-Affluent, the Mega-Affluent, and the Maxi-Affluent

Exhibit 1.3

THE WEALTH OF THE AFFLUENT[1]

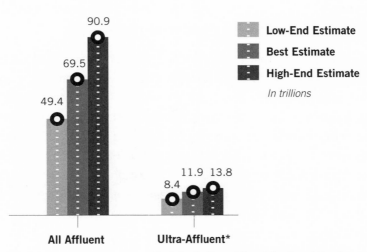

Low-End Estimate
Best Estimate
High-End Estimate
In trillions

All Affluent: 49.4, 69.5, 90.9

Ultra-Affluent*: 8.4, 11.9, 13.8

*Includes the Supra-Affluent, the Mega-Affluent and the Maxi-Affluent

[1] It is important to note that in all of our estimates of assets controlled by the affluent we capped the wealth of the maxi-affluent at $1.2 billion for methodological reasons, though there are clearly many among the ranks of the maxi-affluent who exceeded the cap.

CREATING ULTRA-AFFLUENCE

Becoming a millionaire is certainly far easier than it used to be, in part thanks to inflation. Investment, inheritance, or even years of 401(k) contributions just might just turn the trick these days. But mutual funds and retirement plan rollovers are not going to land anyone in the ultra-affluent class.

As part of the analytic model, we addressed the question of what created the ultra-affluence. We began by extensively documenting the sources of wealth of the supra-affluent, the mega-affluent, and the maxi-affluent and then incorporated the information into our model. As it turned out, developing a significant asset such as a business, stock, or real estate was far and away the most common route to ultra-affluence (Exhibit 1.4). That does not mean that inheritance will not get one there — there are still plenty of American dynasties, including the Rockefellers, Fords, and Mellons. But even among those ultra-affluent flag bearers, the initial path to vast wealth was the development of a significant asset.

Exhibit 1.4

CREATING ULTRA-AFFLUENCE

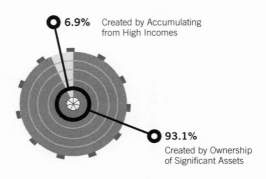

6.9% Created by Accumulating
from High Incomes

93.1%
Created by Ownership
of Significant Assets

Being able to amass more than $25 million without that wealth coming from the building of significant assets is a relatively recent phenomenon, and the remaining seven percent of the ultra-affluent come from such high-profile fields as the entertainment world and financial services. Think of Julia Roberts and George Soros as examples.

SUMMARY

There have never been more rich people in America than there are today, particularly people who have attained the upper reaches of wealth that begin at $25 million. And, in addition to money, members of this ultra-affluent group share something else: an awareness that managing their finances and the issues around them is a full-time job that calls for the work of a team of advisors.

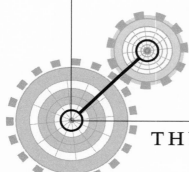

Chapter 2

THE ULTRA-AFFLUENT

As a class and as individuals, the
ultra-affluent are defined — and
best understood — by the interplay
of five core characteristics and
high-net-worth personalities.

LET ME TELL YOU ABOUT THE VERY RICH:

THEY ARE DIFFERENT FROM YOU AND ME.

F. Scott Fitzgerald

The ultra-affluent are distinguished, first and foremost, by their vast wealth, the simple fact that they have lots of money and can spend it as they wish. But our research, confirmed by experience, revealed that they also have in common five core characteristics that relate to the way they think of and use their wealth. The five core characteristics are complexity, control, connections, capital, and charity. Of course, beyond those core characteristics, the ultra-affluent are as distinct and diverse as any large group of individuals. Psychological, social, cultural, and contextual variables all impact individual decision-making. How they were raised, their educational and occupational experiences, their prior history with advisors, their interest in financial matters — all these and more affect their mindset, attitudes about wealth, and their relationships with professional advisors. It is the job of the advanced planner — and, indeed, of any advisor to the wealthy — to understand both the general and specific details of ultra-affluent personalities and to be fully attuned to their similarities as well as their differences.

Nonetheless, we believe that the five core characteristics will provide a sound framework for the way that professional advisors work with the ultra-affluent. In addition, there are five derivative characteristics that should be taken into account. These five derivative characteristics are:

- ∴ Their increasingly demanding nature;
- ∴ The fact that they are driven by profit;
- ∴ That they live in a different world than the "average" person;
- ∴ That they confront the specter of the overclass; and
- ∴ That they are plagued by perceived financial fragility.

Finally, the data on the fundamental, financially-related values of the ultra-affluent will be described and connected to the core values by drawing upon work we have done in applying psychographic analyses to the explication of a financial market segment.

A METHODOLOGICAL NOTE

The findings on the ultra-affluent are based on the industry's single largest and most diverse database of the affluent; that of Prince & Associates. We have systematically collected broad-spectrum data on the affluent and the ultra-affluent, our data covering the wealthy who work with all institutions and all types of financial advisors, including brokers, private bankers, registered investment advisors, financial planners, life insurance professionals, bankers, accountants, attorneys, and family offices. Although the databases of Prince & Associates were culled for empirically derived insights into the ultra-affluent, some limitations due to sample size across studies existed, even using meta-analytic approaches. We therefore combined our empirical research findings with the perceptions and interpretations of leading professional advisors. For this component, we relied on a modified Delphi methodology to ascertain and evaluate key characteristics of the ultra-affluent.

THE FIVE CORE CHARACTERISTICS

We have found the following core characteristics to be emblematic of the ultra-affluent. That is not to say that other economic, social, or cultural populations do not share the characteristics, only that they are more pronounced and impactful among this very wealthy affluent market segment.

COMPLEXITY

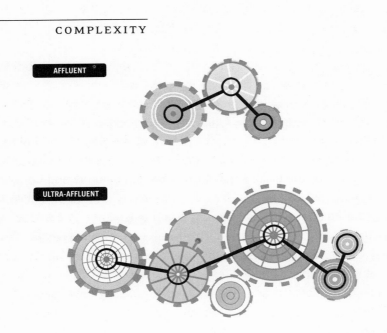

COMPLEXITY Simply stated, the fact that the ultra-affluent have more money makes their personal and financial lives more complicated. External macro-environmental factors such as tax and estate laws naturally play a far larger role in their lives than they do for the less wealthy, and the ultra-affluent are often constrained when it comes to their capital. In fact, the very policies that constrain them also create significant complexity. The current estate and inheritance policy is a good example. Unless a sophisticated level of prior planning is undertaken, estate taxes at the federal and state levels can be substantial. The challenge of investment management is another example of complexity at work. Diversification is relatively easy to achieve with smaller portfolios, but for a multi-million dollar portfolio with global exposure, proper diversification is extremely complex, requiring an intricate balance of investments and tax trade-offs.

The ultra-affluent want to structure their assets to maximize value and ensure preservation, and, along the way, they will confront complicated financial issues ranging from embedded capital gains to, speaking hyperbolically, deciding how much to pay in taxes. Globalization has also produced an environment where many of the ultra-affluent confront tax and related financial issues that are multi-jurisdictional, creating a quagmire of international entanglements.

That goes for ultra-affluent foreign nationals, as well, a highly desirable market segment. Consider the case of the wealthiest segment of the Chinese in Hong Kong. Denied British passports when the colony reverted to the People's Republic of China in 1999, they moved assets by the billions out of Hong Kong. California and Canada were initially big beneficiaries of this transfer of assets, but now a significant amount of that money is returning to China in the form of investments by those families in traditional and new asset areas. The investors are, for example, buying back their traditional lands and reestablishing their businesses (or starting new ones) to take advantage of political and economic restructuring. The back-and-forth creates a maze of legal and tax issues that have to be sorted through, usually requiring the services of professional advisors.

Another area of intense complexity is created by family and personal dealings. The family dynamic is ever-complicated, and money often magnifies eccentricities and animosities. With many voices weighing in, the ultra-affluent often have to settle for accommodation rather than optimization. Keeping peace within a family, for example, can override the best course of action for transferring a family business. There are many, many examples of these family systems that play out in the courtrooms and the pages of the tabloid press. Consider the highly secretive Mars family, still in control of one of the largest privately held businesses in the United States, the Mars candy company. When affections become realigned, so does control over blocks of stock, and family members take positions that put family needs ahead of business considerations.

CONTROL

CONTROL Money and power walk hand in hand, so it is no surprise that the ultra-affluent are often focused on ensuring appropriate levels of control. They want to exercise a measure of control or influence over just about every situation of significance in their lives. By the same token, a healthy ego born of success in the business world or just the raw power of money leads some of the ultra-affluent to believe that their solution to any problem is generally the best way to go.

Needless to say, when the complexity of their lives already referred to meets the need for control head-on, life can be very complicated for the ultra-affluent — and for their professional advisors. When, for example, the objective is the perpetuation of the founding fortune, the strategies and tactics that are employed do more than just ensure the tax-efficient transfer and perpetuation of vast wealth. They also create an emotional and cognitive framework in which the benefactors must live. There is a psychological, if not legal, hold on the benefactors that make many of them quite ambivalent about their situation.

While not going on strike, the ultra-affluent do exert themselves through intricate avoidance and protective behaviors toward the obstacles that society places before them. And they usually turn to professional advisors to assist them. The affluent exert control (and create barriers to uncontrolled contact) by working through armies of advisors. The typical affluent investor has an attorney, an accountant, at least two insurance professionals (property and casualty as well as life), a banker, and an average of three investment advisors. When assets are run through a business, the number of support personnel can grow to the point where whole institutions are involved.

In the end, control is demonstrated by the way that a fortune is structured, communicating just what the wealth creators think of themselves and others, be they family, friends, nonprofits, or the government. Consider the fascination a number of the ultra-affluent have with family incentive trusts, certain types of family limited partnerships, and even the way some family offices are organized. All these strategies and tactics convey the need to be in control.

At the highest end of the ultra-affluent ladder, the need for control can extend beyond mere families and corporations. Witness Ted Turner's $1 billion pledge to the United Nations, which is distributed through a foundation he controls, or the highly selective way that Bill Gates makes charitable contributions. To quote Max Bialystock in Mel Brook's *The Producers*, "If you got it, baby, flaunt it."

CONNECTIONS

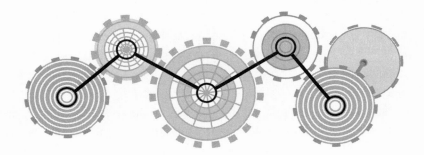

CONNECTIONS   Success for the ultra-affluent is not only about money. The Chinese have a word for it, and that word is *guanxi* — connections. It is sometimes said that with the right *guanxi*, the right connections, almost anything is possible. Among the ultra-affluent the judicious application of their contacts is essential in both personal encounters as well as facilitating their business success. These relationships are highly prized and are therefore well protected.

What is also evident is that, in general, the ultra-affluent have access to significant numbers of influential people. The phrase "six degrees of separation" describes how many nodes on a sociogram a person would need to transcend to meet anyone. However, in the case of the ultra-affluent, we are rarely talking about six nodes. One detailed socio-diagraming of an ultra-affluent familial unit not originating in the United States found that it was able to access 91.3 percent of the local political and business leaders as well as 61.1 percent of Beltway politicians with no more than three degrees of separation. In sum, where the ultra-affluent are concerned, the issue is not only access, but influence. And, in this respect, connections both address their ability to reach out to someone and to get something out of their connections.

CAPITAL

CAPITAL By capital, we do not mean wealth per se, but the way that the ultra-affluent use money to define themselves. Capital, in this context, is the ability to deploy resources to make things happen, that is, not money itself, but what money can accomplish. That may explain why many of the ultra-affluent emphasize the importance of the preservation of wealth — of the maintenance of the power of capital — as opposed to increasing that wealth at the risk of that power. They will only turn their attention to wealth-building when they feel certain that enough wealth is secured to protect their future.

The Ramaz family is an internationally renowned example of the integration of ultra-affluence with capital and personal identity. The way the family deploys its resources in both business ventures and charitable causes reinforces its personal identity. In speaking to members of the Ramaz family, we found that they define themselves based on the way they deploy their wealth, by their use of capital, a mindset similar to senior executives who see themselves reflected in the actions of the company they work for.

CHARITY

CHARITY Public policy in the United States since the early 20th century has been to create tax incentives for philanthropic actions. And those incentives, coupled with the genuine charitable impulse of the ultra-affluent, have a tremendous impact on the nonprofit sector.

Based on our research, we found that the ultra-affluent are not charitable simply because of the tax incentives and the desire to see their name chiseled in stone as benefactors; they are earnestly looking for ways to "make the world a better place." Admittedly, because of the tax breaks, charitable gifting does benefit the ultra-affluent as well as the nonprofit organizations they support. Nevertheless, the ultra-affluent like the sense of purpose charitable gifting gives them and a number aspire to be philanthropists following in the footsteps of Carnegie and Ford. But in fact, the desire to give comes first and only then do taxes affect the tactics and strategies for giving.

The experience of the Soloton Society demonstrates the interplay of charity with the other core characteristics. The Soloton Society works with the high-end of the ultra-affluent, and in the 1990s alone it facilitated nearly $6 billion in charitable gifts worldwide. The Soloton Society has found that the complexity of the personal and financial situations of the ultra-affluent combined with a pervasive desire for control and their self-definition tied to capital results in the preference for private foundations and similar types of charitable gifting strategies.

THE INTERPLAY OF CORE CHARACTERISTICS   As noted, there is rich interplay between the five core characteristics. For example, in the discussion of attitudes towards capital, we noted that the ultra-affluent seek meaningful investment opportunities after they have achieved appropriate levels of capital conservation. Such incremental investment patterns confer additional amounts of control to the investor, and present an even more complicated picture for any financial advisor. In effect, the more money the ultra-affluent have, the more the five core characteristics come into play, increasing the need for advisors and advanced planners who can help insulate the ultra-affluent from their highly complicated financial life yet still reinforce their sense of control. That is a tall order indeed.

DERIVATIVE CHARACTERISTICS

The five core characteristics provide the framework for all of the work that professional advisors do for the ultra-affluent. In addition to the core characteristics, however, there are a number of derivative characteristics that should be taken into account, specifically, the fact that the ultra-affluent are:

∷ Increasingly demanding;

∷ Driven by profit;

∷ Living in a different world than the "average" person;

∷ Confronting the specter of the overclass; and

∷ Plagued by perceived financial fragility.

INCREASINGLY DEMANDING   With money comes many privileges, and working with the best, internationally reputed, professional advisors is — or can certainly be — one of those privileges. When it comes to advanced planning, the ultra-affluent are unquestionably searching for the best as there is a great deal at stake, not to mention, their "identities." The ultra-affluent generally recognize the need to pay top dollar for this level of expertise, and as they are paying top dollar, they expect exceptional expertise.

The corollary of paying for the best is their insistence on getting the best. In effect, the ultra-affluent are more demanding and this trend is only intensifying. By being demanding, the ultra-affluent can become quite difficult as clients because of the complexity of their situations and their need for control.

Aside from paying more and thus wanting more, the ultra-affluent are often more sophisticated clients. Most have many years of experience in managing financial and legal advisors. They, or their army of advisors and kibitzers, can be very critical of the services they receive.

The demands that the ultra-affluent place on their professional advisors are myriad, but one of the most important is technical expertise. The ultra-affluent expect their advisors to personally have (or have on their team) all the requisite expertise they will need to achieve their goals. The ultra-affluent do not expect one person to encompass all the expertise that they may need to call upon, but they do expect a professional advisor to be able to access the requisite expertise when needed.

There are other demands made by the ultra-affluent, including a high, time-intensive, and often exhaustive level of personal attention. That is part of the price that is paid for these profitable relationships. Because of the complexities, need for control, and the intricacies of the family system dynamics mentioned earlier, the ultra-affluent also exact an emotional toll as well, the impact of which some advisors may fail to anticipate.

DRIVEN BY PROFIT   The ultra-affluent want advisors who can deliver profits. This is not only about making money, but more importantly about the way that money stays in their pockets. Avoiding taxes is an obsession with many of the ultra-affluent, which means there is more and more pressure on financial advisors to become profit centers (in all markets) rather than cost centers (due to their fee structures).

The ultra-affluent expect a positive financial return from their professional advisors. They expect positive returns from the allocation of their capital resources in the same way that a bank would, and professional advisors who do not understand this will not remain working with this segment of the high-net-worth market for long.

LIVING IN A DIFFERENT WORLD THAN THE "AVERAGE" PERSON
The social and economic gaps between the "haves" and "have-nots" are as stark today as they were in pre-Revolutionary France before heads began to roll. By experience and design, the ultra-affluent are removed from the societal experiences of the "average" person — recall George Bush Sr.'s astonishment at the use of a supermarket price scanner. This phenomenon is most easily observed in their walled estates, their wealthy enclaves in major metropolitan cities, and even their own islands. Professional advisors have to be aware that the ultra-affluent are often living in a self-created and well-constructed cocoon and they must therefore be treated with especial care and consideration.

CONFRONTING THE SPECTER OF THE OVERCLASS There is no shortage of conspiracy theories in the world today, and one of them posits that the world is ruled by a handful of mysterious billionaires. Such rubbish is nothing new. From the ancient Illuminati and the Priory of Scion right down to the modern Council on Foreign Relations and the Trilateral Commission, some people have long believed in the idea of a secret ruling elite, an overclass that is pulling the strings.

The ultra-affluent do indeed represent a "class," but certainly not an overclass. They comprise a class in the sense that they can be defined by their net-worth and consequently embody certain attitudes and behavioral patterns that are a product of wealth. But the ultra-affluent are far too numerous, far too fragmented geographically and ethnically, and far too divided in their politics to constitute an overclass. While this is the reality, the specter of the overclass can sometimes haunt the ultra-affluent as might be the case when a charitable gesture is met with the suspicion of an ulterior motive.

PLAGUED BY PERCEIVED FINANCIAL FRAGILITY As surely as fortunes have been made, they have been lost. A sharp downturn in the stock market, for instance, could deal a body blow to the net-worth of someone who is over-exposed on the equity side. Fortunes can also be squandered without any outside help if family members engage in speculative excess. And there are other threats, including family feuds and outside litigation. The ultra-affluent do not want to lose their money and the social standing it gives many of them. And the ultra-affluent have a far higher ceiling than most — to them, dropping from $50 million to $25 million could be seen as a disaster. Once someone has gotten used to being very well off, being merely wealthy can be hard to abide. It is incumbent on the professional advisor, therefore, to not only take the financial steps necessary to ensure than a high level of wealth is, at the very least, maintained, but also to reassure the ultra-affluent that they will not soon fall from their pedestals and end up mingling with the hoi polloi or even garden variety millionaires.

THE HIGH-NET-WORTH PERSONALITIES

The ultra-affluent, as seen through the prism of their five core characteristics, constitute a distinct market segment. But when it comes to money, there are many different high-net-worth personalities for professional advisors to contend with, and ignoring them would recall the unprincipled certainty of Procrustes.

Procrustes was a mythical thief of ancient Attica. He solved the problem of individual differences by ensuring the body of his victims conformed to the length of his bed. This feat was accomplished with a saw for the tall victims and a rack for the shorter ones. The moral for today's professional advisors is that it is wise to have a number of different size beds to offer.

By understanding the differences among the ultra-affluent, professional advisors are better able to create the types of relationships that result in success for both parties. Therefore, we will now turn to psychographics in order to understand how the ultra-affluent look at both their assets and their professional advisors.

The creation of psychographic segments — or personalities — involved using the multidimensional statistical tools of factor and cluster analysis on the body of data collected on affluent purchasers of financial services and products. Since factor analysis is the understanding of constructs or concepts that groups of individuals share in a greater or lesser degree, and since cluster analysis groups customer on the basis of their relative homogeneity, these two techniques in combination allow us to illuminate how each high-net-worth personality is motivated to buy and use financial services — in particular advanced planning services — as well as the way that they want to partner with their advisors. And high-net-worth psychology enables professional advisors to better connect with their ultra-affluent clients.

The following provides an overview of the nine high-net-worth personalities and some of their key attributes.

Exhibit 2.1

THE HIGH-NET-WORTH PERSONALITIES

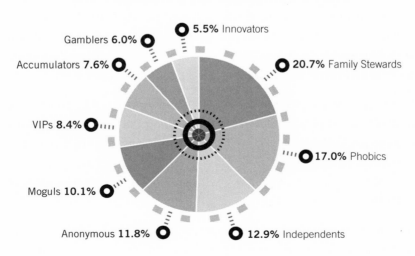

5.5% Innovators

Gamblers 6.0%

Accumulators 7.6%

20.7% Family Stewards

VIPs 8.4%

17.0% Phobics

Moguls 10.1%

Anonymous 11.8%

12.9% Independents

FAMILY STEWARDS.............................20.7%
- Want to use their wealth to care for their family.
- Want to relieve their family members of financial worries.
- Want to take care of their personal obligations.

PHOBICS 17.0%
- Hate being involved in financial decisions.
- Not knowledgeable about financial matters.
- Dislike discussing investing.

INDEPENDENTS...............................12.9%
- See attention to financial issues as a necessary evil.
- Want personal freedom.
- Want to have a safety net if they bail out.

ANONYMOUS 11.8%
- Confidentiality concerning financial matters is key.
- Secretive about their financial dealings.
- Financial success is essential for personal comfort.

MOGULS......................................10.1%
- Financial success is a way of keeping score and winning.
- Wealth brings power.
- Seek personal influence.

VIPS...8.4%
- Financial success is a way to achieve high status.
- Want to be well known.
- Seek prestige.

ACCUMULATORS 7.6%
- Their top goal is asset accumulation.
- Can't be too rich.
- Their sole objective is to make money.

GAMBLERS 6.0%
- Treat dealing with financial matters as a hobby.
- Derive pleasure from the machinations of the markets.
- They relish the investing process.

INNOVATORS...................................5.5%
- Perceive investing to be a challenge.
- Want to be on the cutting edge of financial technology.
- Want to be employing state-of-the-art strategies and tactics.

(Source: *Cultivating the Affluent, Institutional Investor*; 1995.)

FAMILY STEWARDS   Family Stewards, the most prevalent high-net-worth personalities, are deceptively simple: they are motivated by the need to protect their families over the long-term. This motivation makes them suitable candidates for a wide range of financial services. Research reveals, however, that there is a complex interplay of psychological factors to contend with. That is because Family Stewards are not only characterized by a high degree of internal control — or the confidence to control their own fate and fortune — but also by a deep distrust of the world.

Family Stewards fear for the safety of their families and they are highly motivated to organize defenses against external threats. This interplay of the themes of safety and threat have operational implications, implying that Family Stewards can be relatively difficult to approach because a new advisor will often be perceived as an "outsider." This prediction is borne out by data from the field.

PHOBICS   The second most prevalent high-net-worth personality is typified by people who, although they are wealthy, dislike thinking about money. This personality also has significant control issues because they do not think they are capable of managing their own financial affairs. While this mindset is relatively pervasive among the high-net-worth personalities, it is extreme in the case of the Phobics. However, Phobics also believe they are not especially capable of effectively managing the advisors they turn to for assistance.

This deep feeling of being out of control over this important aspect of their lives makes this segment suspicious and off-putting. Like Family Stewards, they can be difficult to approach and, when won as clients, they can be hard to manage.

INDEPENDENTS   This high-net-worth personality includes people whose primary objective in accumulating assets is to achieve financial independence and the accompanying security. Some want to retire to pursue other activities. Others will continue to be involved but value the security of knowing they could leave at any time.

These ultra-affluent have a high degree of internal control and they are indifferent to a broad range of external threats if they can be protected from them. In contrast to the other high-net-worth personalities, they believe the world is a relatively benign place. Independents are also very open to advanced planning if it is tied to their fundamental goals and beliefs.

THE ANONYMOUS   This high-net-worth personality shares with the Family Stewards a distrust of external forces, but to an even greater degree. Anonymous ultra-affluent clients are typified by their deep-seated — and sometimes irrational — need for privacy and confidentiality in all of their financial as well as selected personal dealings.

In their interior belief system, they fear that the disclosure of information will enable someone or some office to get control over them and their affairs. As a result, they are often unwilling to disclose their affairs, even to "trusted" financial advisors. This makes them particularly difficult to engage in advanced planning services unless a very high level of rapport is established.

MOGULS   The ultra-affluent with this personality are motivated to accumulate more and more assets in order to achieve personal power (and, by extension, influence if not control). In short, they want to leverage the power conferred by wealth.

Moguls are moderate in terms of optimism/pessimism and introversion/extroversion. From professional advisors, they require an acknowledgement of their power. Importantly, they are motivated to participate in advanced planning services that will demonstrably increase their power.

VIPS   The people with this high-net-worth personality are motivated to accumulate assets and utilize their wealth, in part to achieve greater status and prestige. This personality prizes the opinion of select others above all else. They are, as a result, more likely to purchase the external symbols of wealth than any other high-net-worth personality. They see such symbols, including jets and private islands, as badges of their exalted status.

This high-net-worth personality is less certain about personal control, and thus relies more on external resources. They are also comparatively fearful, worrying about threats to their wealth and status. For professional advisors, the job is twofold: reassure them while remaining optimistic about their finances, and also exhibit deference and regard for their status.

ACCUMULATORS This high-net-worth personality seeks to accumulate assets out of an overriding concern for personal financial well-being. Unlike other high-net-worth personalities, Accumulators do not seek to achieve family security or emblems of wealth or power. Instead, their focus is on the continual accumulation and protection of assets as a bulwark against an uncertain future.

Accumulators tend to see threats to their financial well-being from all sides. In addition, people with this high-net-worth personality do not have a great deal of confidence in their ability to achieve either internal or external control.

GAMBLERS Gamblers are high on both internal and external control dimensions. They believe their skills and competence will protect them from all significant threats, they are self-reliant, and they are more inclined to be extroverted.

They view financial affairs as a personal challenge, but one that they are very capable of handling. For instance, in the investment management world, they seek "playmates," people to share their enthusiasm with, and they are by nature optimistic. They look to professional advisors to maximize their self-image (i.e., capital) and help them realize complete control and protection over their asset pool.

INNOVATORS Innovators are moderately high on both internal and external control dimensions. They believe their analytical capabilities will sustain them and protect them from external threats. And, because of their life-long reliance on their analytic capabilities, they are highly self-reliant and do not delegate any portion of life tasks having to do with analysis.

Unlike Gamblers, they are more inclined to be introverted. They view financial affairs as an analytic challenge and they look for professionals who will feed them useful information as well as facilitate implementation, avoiding those who try and dominate them without understanding their analytical bent. Innovators who want to understand every detail of financial models will regularly challenge professional advisors. Professional advisors working with this personality need to empathize with their essential values, as well as their belief in control and their proclivity for minute analysis.

THE HIGH-NET-WORTH PERSONALITIES AND CORE CHARACTERISTICS

These various frameworks overlap and interplay. Certainly there is much to learn from examining the five core characteristics of the ultra-affluent alongside the psychographic segmentation. That meta-framework is created when the two are crossed, as illustrated in the table below (Exhibit 2.2).

We can see that each of the psychographic segments has different complexity, control, connections, capital, and charitable attributes and needs. For example, professional financial advisors working with Family Stewards will find the situation very complex because of the overlay of the family system on the asset system (usually the privately held business). By contrast, the complexity of working with Phobics is magnified by their inattention to financial affairs and the difficulties of extracting financial information from them.

To extend the example, consider the second column, control. Family Stewards who are in control of the assets are generally reluctant to yield that control to either advisors or to the succeeding generation (which is why estate planning with this group can be notoriously difficult). Among Phobics, however, control plays out differently.

Phobics do not want to be in control over their assets; instead, they are seeking a person or persons they can trust to manage their assets on their behalf.

Connections are a less well-understood attribute of the ultra-wealthy, but may be the most critical to professional advisors. Connections, as noted, are the network of social and professional relationships through which people move. Connections are the supporting social web of human existence. From the perspective of the professional advisor, connections are part of the future ROI of a client relationship because connections represent the potential incremental business obtainable by referral from each type of client.

Both Family Stewards and Phobics are charitably motivated. However, the former sees philanthropy as a means to improve the world on behalf of their children. Charity also gives Family Stewards a mechanism to transfer their values to the next generation. For these reasons Family Stewards are usually intimately involved in the charitable gifting process. This is in direct contrast to Phobics who expect results but choose not to be involved in the financial and legal maneuvering necessary to attain these results.

Exhibit 2.2

THE INTERPLAY OF THE CORE CHARACTERISTICS
AND THE HIGH-NET-WORTH PERSONALITIES

HIGH-NET-WORTH PERSONALITY	COMPLEXITY	CONTROL	CONNECTIONS	CAPITAL	CHARITY
Family Stewards	Family political dynamics significant	Current controlling generation resists succession	Principal connections are family ties easiest to leverage horizontally	Need to maintain family control over the business	Desire to make a better world for their children
Phobics	Difficult to manage information flow with this segment	Seeking to replace control with trust	Well qualified social network of peers	Highly oriented towards conservation of capital	Want results without attending to financial and legal details
Independents	Complex because not always available for decision-making	Seek control over personal activities and autonomy	Prefers few good friends and business associates to many acquaintances	Conservation of capital needs outweigh investments	Tied to instruments that help them assure their goal of personal financial independence
Anonymous	Difficult to manage security concerns	Need highest control over privacy and confidentiality	Network limited but tight	Privacy needs drive financial decision-making	Seek to preserve anonymity in giving
Moguls	Will tolerate complexity in planning and management	Highest control needs of all of the segments	Network focused downward so power can be exerted	Highly oriented towards new investments (more control opportunities)	Another avenue they can use to exert power and influence
VIPs	Need for public recognition creates complexity	Need control over personal persona and reputation	Network focused upward in direction of aspiration, social ties shallower	Will invest in vehicles that create public image	Another avenue for status, prestige, and public recognition
Accumulators	Vast and diverse holdings create complex situations	Demand high levels of control and frequent reporting	Medium network, heterogeneous in character	Will accept investment if capital conservation objectives met	Not highly charitably oriented
Gamblers	Complexity created by need for intense communications and quick reaction time	Seeking a wide variety of opportunities, not control	Moderate network characterized by intense interaction and shared passions	Most risk-tolerant of all segments, highly investment oriented	Often directly connected to financial returns
Innovators	Very technically demanding, requiring complex solutions	Will not relinquish control over advanced planning	On introverted side, limited social network, concentrated	Will trade off capital conservation for investment	Interested in new financial solutions as well as creative programs

SUMMARY

Understanding the ultra-affluent is a daunting task — but an essential one for the professional advisors who work with them. Our research has revealed five core characteristics — complexity, control, connections, capital, and charity — that are endemic to this affluent class. These core characteristics interact, and in so doing provide the framework for the way that professional advisors should work with the ultra-affluent. In addition, there are derivative characteristics that should be taken into account. Finally, professional advisors should decide which of the nine high-net-worth personalities their clients possess. Only then can they fully understand, manage, and meet the high expectations of their ultra-affluent clients.

Part II

ADVANCED
PLANNING

To succeed with ultra-affluent clients, professional advisors must have a comprehensive advanced planning process in place that begins with information gathering and continues on beyond implementation to seamlessly accommodate any updates or amendments to the plan. Just as importantly, advisors must be able to connect with their clients every step of the way during that process on both a personal and professional level, while understanding that each client has a unique set of circumstances and concerns that need to be addressed.

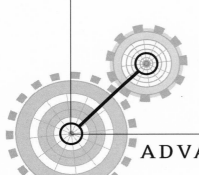

Chapter 3

THE NATURE OF
ADVANCED PLANNING

Advanced planning for the ultra-affluent is a lucrative field of endeavor, but success requires advisors who have exceptional interpersonal skills, vast technical knowledge and resources, and, most importantly, the ability to effectively package and deliver that knowledge on a client-by-client basis.

NOTHING IN PROGRESSION

CAN REST ON ITS ORIGINAL PLAN.

WE MAY AS WELL THINK OF ROCKING A GROWN MAN

IN THE CRADLE OF AN INFANT.

Edmund Burke

Advanced planning is the essential task of the professional advisor. Without the interaction fostered by advanced planning, advisors would not know enough about their ultra-affluent clients to properly assess each client's needs and wants. Without planning, the advisor would not be able to translate those needs and wants into goals and be sure that those goals are being met. And without a well articulated and well executed planning process, ultra-affluent clients would not know whether or not their advisor is effectively addressing their wants and needs and pragmatically meeting their goals.

Advanced planning is the process through which a professional advisor and an ultra-affluent client ensure that they are on the same page strategically. The process enables both parties to reveal more about themselves and the way they like to work. Along the way, advanced planning creates a level of security and comfort that is the foundation for a long-term, mutually profitable relationship. Advanced planning is also a critical process for professional advisors because it is how they can locate and reposition the assets of an ultra-affluent client to best achieve the client's goals and objectives.

The central aspect of advanced planning to the ultra-affluent is, of course, the advisor. As noted in the previous chapter, the challenges facing the ultra-affluent are extremely complex, and very few advisors are capable of working effectively in these upper reaches of affluence. Professional advisors who are expert at advanced planning employ a variety of strategies and tactics to meet the specific objectives and goals of their ultra-affluent clients, which vary dramatically depending on an individual client's age, situation, and psychographic profile.

While the ultra-affluent client sets the parameters for the relationship, the professional advisor can — and should — manage the client's expectations.

In order to best meet the needs, wants and explore the possibilities available to the ultra-affluent, advanced planning must be conceptualized as a set of services, a methodology for applying these services, and as way of creating "de facto uniqueness" for this level of private wealth.

BASIC VS. STATE OF THE ART

The strategies and tactics of professional advisors can be characterized as basic and state of the art. The basics include the plethora of tools, techniques, and products that are readily recognized and generally applicable for most clients, including the wealthier ones. Consider the case of variable life insurance. For many people, irrespective of the level of affluence, obtaining a variable life insurance policy may be a wise decision whether it is used to create or to maintain an estate. Most advisors will be able to effectively guide clients when it comes to their decision as to whether or not they should get a variable life policy and also help them understand the role it plays as a result of their financial profile. A private placement variable life insurance policy is a very different matter. Here we are entering the realm of state of the art, and few advisors are expert in the nuances and intricacies of private placement variable life. Yet many ultra-affluent clients are excellent candidates for this product. To thrive, an advisor working with the ultra-affluent will therefore have to understand state-of-the-art financial products. (For a more detailed discussion of private placement variable life insurance see **Chapter 5: To the Edge**.)

Of course, clients must have enough money to make state-of-the-art tactics and strategies viable. With respect to private placement variable life insurance, for example, the client must be an accredited or a qualified investor. While this does not always translate into the client being ultra-affluent, it does mean that they are two standard deviations above the mean as defined by either income or net-worth. In short, state-of-the-art products and strategies are explicitly designed to solve specific problems of the high-net-worth segment.

THE EVOLUTION OF A
STATE-OF-THE-ART PRODUCT

Over the past several decades, there has been significant work on the ways in which state-of-the-art innovations are created and disseminated. These models can be applied to the financial services industry quite readily and provide a sold framework for this analysis. Naturally, most innovations are solutions to new problems. In the financial services industry, the innovations are typically designed to benefit the ultra-affluent because they are the ones with enough money to draw the special attention of financial and legal institutions, as well as professional advisors with the power and resources to create new products to meet their needs. New strategies, tactics, and products in the financial services industry increasingly start with the ultra-affluent or even approaches certain corporations might pursue in order to mitigate taxes. The ultra-affluent are generally looking to take a more judiciously aggressive approach and are positioned to better leverage the tax and related laws and regulations, driving the demand for new solutions (and hence, new strategies and tactics). A variety of derivative instruments, for instance, were created as ways for wealthy clients to offset investment risks. At this initial stage, there is a great deal of experimentation going on as a handful of state-of-the-art tactics and products are tweaked for highly specialized client situations.

After having used the product or tactic in several situations, professional advisors will begin to see that some of these customized solutions might be useful for other similarly affluent clients. In this way, strategy and tactic templates begin to be formed, with substantial customization still possible for major client situations. Products that had been uniquely developed are now being "productized" for a larger market.

If these products continued to be successful, full productization occurs and a field sales force is mobilized to introduce them to a wider market, armed with sales brochures and off-the-shelf supporting software. Because the products are fully designed — in effect, much more turnkey — they can be sold by advisors who are less proficient than the professional advisors who were instrumental in bringing the product to life. In the final stage, decline, products are beginning to be supplanted by newer, innovative products working their way through the system.

Exhibit 3.1

LIFE CYCLE OF FINANCIAL PRODUCTS

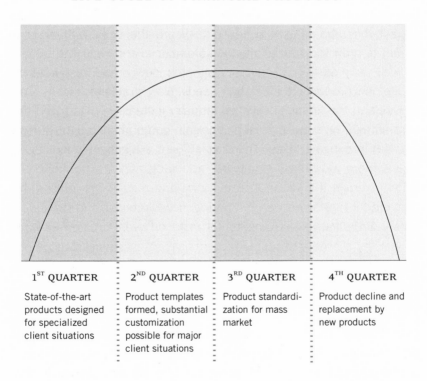

1ST QUARTER	2ND QUARTER	3RD QUARTER	4TH QUARTER
State-of-the-art products designed for specialized client situations	Product templates formed, substantial customization possible for major client situations	Product standardization for mass market	Product decline and replacement by new products

A YARDSTICK FOR JUDGING ADVISORS

For the ultra-affluent, there are several yardsticks for assessing professional advisors, including their understanding and use of state-of-the-art strategies and tactics, their ability to comprehend the effects of any action on the overall planning picture, and being able to use professional relationships to optimize results. Relatively few advisors are able to work at the cutting edge and integrate what they find there with the other pieces of the whole — and those who can are the drivers of change in the industry.

The ultra-affluent will, in concert with their professional advisors, need to determine their goals and consequently the best course of action. While the ultra-affluent are not adept at discerning what specific strategies and tactics to use, they will need to understand in broad brush strokes what the consequences of each action will be. And in some cases, the basics may be sufficient. A mastery of the basics is a given for advisors working with the ultra-affluent. In a fair percentage of cases, in fact, there is no need to move beyond the basics. In such instances, the advisor's cutting-edge expertise is not needed, but their judgement and ability to see the client's best course of action are of considerable value.

THE FOUR SERVICES OF ADVANCED PLANNING

Advanced planning entails leveraging the legal, tax, and regulatory systems to provide one or more of the following four interrelated services:

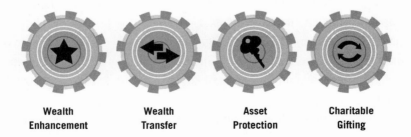

| Wealth Enhancement | Wealth Transfer | Asset Protection | Charitable Gifting |

These four sets of services interlock thematically and are important to varying degrees to ultra-affluent clients depending on each client's high-net-worth personality.

WEALTH ENHANCEMENT

With respect to investment management, the goal is to produce the best possible performance. The ultra-affluent, because they are willing to pay for advice and because they have a lot of money to invest, are clearly focused on returns. Unlike institutional investors such as pension funds and endowments, the ultra-affluent must also contend with taxes, and working to make the tax issues less of a drain on absolute returns is an important aspect of wealth enhancement. The key is for the ultra-affluent, guided by their professional advisors, to determine the current timing, character, and amount of taxable income (often investment income).

When it comes to investment income, the ideal transition is from income to short-term capital gains, to long-term capital gains, to tax deferral, and ultimately to no taxes whatsoever. This continuum drives professional advisor services, with the goal of moving the client situation as far along the continuum as is practicable under the given circumstances.

There are a wide variety of strategies and tactics that can be utilized to enhance wealth. At the current time, some of the most attractive strategies incorporate private placement variable life insurance. Similarly, the "cashless collar" is also in wide demand today. Here the ultra-affluent client can ensure against the loss of current gains on an appreciated security while maintaining some further appreciation potential and retaining some flexibility as to when to take those gains. Another example of a wealth enhancement strategy that has been used in the ultra-affluent market is a contingent swap designed to offset ordinary income and convert it into capital gains over a specified time.

Other examples of wealth enhancement include active portfolio tax management, tax-free environments that can produce tax-free income distributions, prepaid forwards, exchange funds, and, if the ultra-affluent client is charitably inclined, a variety of options including donor-advised funds, charitable remainder trusts, and charitable lead trusts, all of which provide tax deductions as well as other benefits.

Professional advisors are able to significantly enhance wealth when the client's business interests can be integrated, as would be the case in SERP's, SERP swaps, dormant asset financing, synthetic equity used in conjunction with an ESOP, and a number of tax-favored programs that move money and/or benefits from the business to the individual.

WEALTH TRANSFER

As long as there are estate taxes, as long as there are inter-generational considerations, and as long as there are interconnected business interests, there will be a need for wealth transfer strategies and tactics. When it comes to wealth transfer, professional advisors are called upon to not only facilitate the transfer of wealth in accord-ance with the wishes of the ultra-affluent client, but to do so in as tax-efficient a manner as possible.

It is quite possible, for example, to eliminate estate taxes. Achieving that goal could require the use of charitable instruments and formal abrogation of control over selected assets, but the great majority of the ultra-affluent clients are not in the habit of ceding control over many aspects of their lives.

Basic estate planning employing such strategies as credit-shelter trusts and traditional life insurance is far from complicated and sufficient for some ultra-affluent clients. For those clients with a more complicated financial picture and goals, there are a number of more sophisticated approaches to wealth transfer, including self-canceling installment notes, GRAT's, and remainder purchase marital trusts. Centimillionaires, for example, can use a combination of techniques including dynasty trusts to avoid estate taxes forever.

Irrespective of the planning service, the professional advisor's first job is to learn as much as possible about the client and his or her goals. That calls for wisdom, an understanding of human nature, and experience. It should never be taken for granted that the goal of wealth transfer is the most tax-efficient way of passing assets down to the succeeding generation(s). Taxes are not the tail that should wag the dog.

Wealth transfer is an uncomfortable subject for many of the ultra-affluent, but a necessary one if their assets are to be distributed as they would like. Professional advisors can help their ultra-affluent clients confront the disturbing personal task of estate planning by first attending to their own lifetime wants and then showing them the benefits in a way they can understand and at a pace that is comfortable. This has to do with connecting each client's high-net-worth personality with their wealth transfer goals, as we shall see later in this chapter.

ASSET PROTECTION

Asset protection planning, a subset of risk management, is what protects the ultra-affluent's wealth. There are a great many tactics and strategies that the ultra-affluent can employ to protect their wealth against potential creditors and litigants, children-in-law, and potential ex-spouses. Which ones work best can prove to be very situational. In fact, the success of an asset protection strategy is often a function of the sophistication and cunning of the opposition.

Moving beyond the astute use of property and liability insurance, some of the strategies are quite rudimentary and predicated on dissociation (otherwise known as, "I don't own it"). That occurs when the ultra-affluent transfer their assets to another person or entity while retaining access. Such tactics include transferring assets to a spouse and many iterations of offshore trusts and self-settled spendthrift trusts. The law is somewhat developed around the latter as evidenced by the Uniform Fraudulent Transfers Act which has mitigated their value.

Transformation is among the more sophisticated strategies. With transformation, the assets of the ultra-affluent are converted into different assets that are much harder if not impossible for creditors and litigants to acquire because the assets are protected by state bankruptcy laws. The homestead exemption, interests in limited partnerships or limited liability companies, and the selective use of life insurance and annuities are all examples of transformation.

Monetization in conjunction with transformation and replication are at the very cutting edge of asset protection strategies. Monetization strategies utilize forward contracts and complex installment sales, whereas replication strategies benefit from derivatives to make assets disappear and subsequently reappear in entities beyond the reach of creditors or litigants.

CHARITABLE GIFTING

As previously mentioned, charitable gifting can be of great importance to the ultra-affluent. Apart from wealth and success, a strong majority of the ultra-affluent want to give something back (and many also want to enjoy the prestige and visibility that goes with giving). The Carnegie, Ford, Mellon, and Rockefeller foundations have set a precedent that is being followed by today's ultra-affluent, including Bill Gates, Ted Turner, and George Soros. Schools, hospitals, cultural institutions, and religious organizations all have benefactors, many of whom have their names prominently featured in brass and granite. Charitable gifting can also be motivated by those who share Warren Buffet's philosophy of leaving children "enough money so they would feel they could do anything, but not so much that they could do nothing."

While the motivations and values differ, charitable gifting is an important component in advanced planning, especially when coordinated with the other three sets of services. Private foundations are a case in point. A family foundation serves a wide variety of functions but the transfer of wealth between family members is tangential, if applicable at all. Still, research clearly shows the enormous interest among the ultra-affluent in private foundations for a number of reasons having nothing to do with passing on assets to heirs. Thus, professional advisors must incorporate family foundations into the estate plans of many ultra-affluent clients even though they do not result in the transfer of the estate to other family members.

When an ultra-affluent client is strongly philanthropic, that inclination can be coordinated to produce additional wealth enhancement and wealth transfer strategies. Aside from private foundations with their specific limitations, foundations and donor-advised funds allow for the maximum immediate tax benefits timed for the benefit of the ultra-affluent client without the client having to decide which charities will ultimately benefit, or when. Charitable remainder trusts and charitable gift annuities provide both tax benefits and income streams. Charitable lead trusts can be used to finesse the estate tax while passing wealth to future generations. Finally, although philanthropy does not coordinate strongly with asset protection, seeing assets go to charities rather than to litigants and creditors may produce some satisfaction.

ADVANCED PLANNING SERVICES
AND HIGH-NET-WORTH PSYCHOLOGY

In the previous chapter, we introduced high-net-worth psychology, a methodology that has repeatedly been shown to enable advisors targeting the affluent to better understand their needs and wants while more powerfully positioning services and products to them. With respect to advanced planning, the various psychographic segments of the ultra-affluent significantly differ in their interest, the level of detail they require, and their likely aggressiveness in using and implementing the four sets of services (Exhibit 3.2).

FAMILY STEWARDS Ultra-affluent Family Stewards are driven by their goals of safeguarding their families and protecting their families down through the years. They often take a multigenerational point of view, so wealth transfer is more important than wealth enhancement. Asset protection does mesh with the goal of safeguarding the family, so it is a higher priority need. Charitable gifting is also a priority because Family Stewards see nonprofit organizations as vehicles for "making the world a better place" for their children.

PHOBICS Not surprisingly, ultra-affluent Phobics have a far different profile. Because they are "afraid," they do not understand their wealth position, making them a challenging group for professional advisors. Since they neither know much, nor care to know much, about their financial affairs, wealth enhancement is not usually a top priority. They are often unwilling to address wealth transfer issues for the same reasons. Because they are fearful of the loss of their wealth, however, asset protection is highest on their agenda. Phobics are often already quite involved with charities as a psychological and social outlet and they are by-and-large inclined to want to support nonprofits. They are not, however, interested in having to deal with the complexities of major and planned gifts and the impact of such giving on the advanced planning process.

INDEPENDENTS Ultra-affluent Independents present yet another profile. They attach a moderate priority to wealth enhancement because it contributes to their goal of financial and personal independence. For the same reasons, they attach a lower priority to wealth transfer to the extent that the wealth transfer strategies or tactics result in the transfer of control over these assets. Consistent with their goal of autonomy, ultra-affluent Independents prize asset protection services. Because the goal of Independents is personal freedom, they are not inclined to become overly involved with charitable institutions and, in any case, they are not especially motivated to part with the assets they think they will need to achieve their goals.

ANONYMOUS Among the ultra-affluent Anonymous, wealth enhancement is secondary to wealth protection because they are highly motivated to shield their money as well as their identity. They are interested in numerous wealth transfer strategies and tactics as long as their intentions and actions can be masked. For the Anonymous, there is also great interest in asset protection. They are as likely to give as any other segment, and may or may not find the concept interesting for idiosyncratic reasons. For them, however, giving is tempered by the need for anonymity and confidentiality.

MOGULS Ultra-affluent Moguls believe that wealth equals power, and power is both their motivation and goal. Wealth enhancement, therefore, is an especially high priority. Because they are fearful of losing control, wealth transfer is relatively less appealing. Again, because of their hunger for power, asset protection is also a priority because it helps them maintain their social standing. If charitable gifting is positioned as a way to extend personal and social power, Moguls become highly interested.

VIPs For their part, ultra-affluent VIPs believe that wealth is synonymous with respect and prestige, their driving goals. They are seldom motivated to transfer wealth because they fear that doing so would result in a loss of their hard-won status. Among VIPs, asset protection is equated with protection of their position in life and society. They are highly motivated to make charitable contributions as part of the advanced planning process because they readily under-stand that visible acts of philanthropy enhance their status and prestige.

ACCUMULATORS   The top goal for ultra-affluent Accumulators is to increase their assets with wealth enhancement strategies. A lower priority is wealth transfer because they generally do not want to share their wealth; sharing is at odds with accumulation. Asset protection is a high priority because it correlates with their goals. For all these reasons, charitable giving is generally not a major goal of Accumulators as it often runs counter to their personal driver of asset accumulation; in other words, their need to feel safe behind their wall of assets is greater than their desire to give something back.

GAMBLERS   The Gamblers thrive on the excitement and thrills associated with investing and other financial decision-making. They are highly motivated to work with advisors promoting wealth enhancement strategies because that feels like winning. Gamblers are not especially motivated to focus on transferring assets, however, so advisors should not overly promote wealth transfer strategies. Asset protection can also be inconsistent with the risk-taking mentality typical of Gamblers, so positioning is all the more critical. As for charity, Gamblers have to see the charity itself as exciting and compelling.

INNOVATORS   For ultra-affluent Innovators, the top priority is being up on state-of-the-art approaches to managing their financial affairs. When it comes to wealth enhancement, they are most interested and motivated to learn of new approaches. Wealth transfer is a somewhat lower priority with this group while asset protection is of moderate priority, though, in each case, they are interested in new and creative approaches. Innovators are motivated to engage in charitable giving because of its innate appeal and, moreover, become much more involved if the solution is technically interesting and innovative and they believe their approach is state of the art.

Exhibit 3.2

ADVANCED PLANNING SERVICES
AND THE HIGH-NET-WORTH PSYCHOLOGY

HIGH-NET-WORTH PERSONALITY	WEALTH ENHANCEMENT	WEALTH TRANSFER	ASSET PROTECTION	CHARITABLE GIFTING
Family Stewards	Not the top motivation	Very high priority, mesh with goal of safeguarding family	High priority, so family future is secured	High priority, where the family is directly involved
Phobics	Not a top priority, often do not understand wealth position	Commonly unwilling to address transfer issues	Fearful of loss of wealth, making this their top goal	Medium-to-high priority because of their charitable involvement
Independents	Moderate priority, contributes to goal of independence	Lower priority for this segment	Highly consistent with their goal of autonomy	Low priority, impedes achieving top personal goals
Anonymous	Secondary goal to wealth protection	Interested insofar as intent can be veiled when appropriate	Highly motivated to shield money, identity	Moderate, if confidentiality needs can be met
Moguls	Believe wealth equals power, a top goal	May be fearful of losing control via wealth transfer	A priority, to maintain position	Moderate-to-high, a way of expressing power
VIPs	Believe wealth equals respect and prestige, a top goal	Not highly motivated to transfer wealth, fear loss of status	Wealth protection equated with protection of position	High, achieves goal of status and external regard
Accumulators	Top goal for those motivated to maximize asset values	Lower priority, do not generally want to share wealth	Higher priority, drives asset accumulation goals	Low priority as primary focus is on personal safety
Gamblers	Highly motivated, enhancement is winning	Not generally motivated to transfer assets	Inconsistent with risk-taking mentality, requires adroit positioning	Moderate priority if the cause is seen to be exciting
Innovators	Top priority, interested in new approaches	Lower priority, interested in new approaches	Moderate priority, interested in new approaches	High priority, looking for sophisticated ways to leverage their gifts

THE EIGHT CORE ELEMENTS
OF ADVANCED PLANNING

The preceding sections have discussed the core components of advanced planning — wealth enhancement, wealth transfer, asset protection, and charitable gifting. We have also seen how the different high-net-worth personalities of the ultra-affluent prioritize these core components. There are further considerations in advanced planning, however, and those of the utmost importance are the criteria that can predict success for the professional advisor — the eight core elements of advanced planning. Advanced planning must be:

∷ Flexible

∷ Discreet

∷ Transparent

∷ Coherent

∷ Risk-sensitive

∷ Cost-effective

∷ Complexity-sensitive

∷ Legitimate

These eight elements operate in concert with each other (Exhibit 3.3) and must be considered in any ultra-affluent client situation. In fact, the more seasoned and successful professional advisors working with the ultra-affluent have developed a high degree of ingrained competency that is a result of continually working with and thinking about these core elements, which we will now examine in greater detail.

Exhibit 3.3

THE EIGHT CORE ELEMENTS

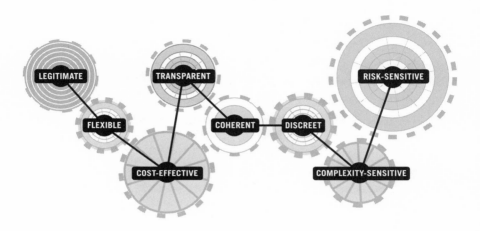

FLEXIBLE Advanced planning must be able to change or adapt in order to meet the exigencies of an evolving situation involving a client's circumstances and/or the financial and legal environments. When it comes to that environment, it is inescapable that laws and regulations will be changed, so successful advanced planners have to not only be flexible and informed, but they also have to think through a range of advanced planning scenarios that anticipate those changing circumstances and laws. (For details on one methodology that enhances flexibility, see **Appendix 2** on page 175, Scenario Thinking.)

DISCREET A high degree of discretion is a prerequisite for any advisor involved with the ultra-affluent. Discretion relates to the nature and details of the interpersonal relationship that is established between advisor and client. Furthermore, though an advisor's strategies and tactics are legitimate and lawful, a low profile helps avoid any questions. Measured discretion also helps the ultra-affluent stay off the radar screens of the United States and foreign governments and their tax authorities, as well as potential litigants and creditors. Professional advisors must always presume that every scrap of paper, every formal communication, and every conversation could be scrutinized. In some areas, the advisor who is not an attorney should remove him or herself so that an attorney handles sensitive areas directly without the advisor being present. In that way, the ultra-affluent client is protected by attorney-client privilege. Sometimes, the professional advisor may even be the attorney's client. The odds against such scrutiny for a legitimate business are substantial, but an emphasis on discretion ensures that even under the most hostile conditions, the client is afforded maximum protection.

TRANSPARENT   Although there is no interest or benefit for anyone to advertise the intricacies of an advanced plan, the plan should nonetheless be made as transparent as possible. As previously noted, advanced planning is not about hiding or laundering monies; it is about leveraging laws and regulations for the benefit of the ultra-affluent. And while confidentiality agreements are often and justifiably used in advanced planning, they do not eliminate the need for transparence. Such agreements are intended to maintain first-mover advantages for the professional advisor as long as possible. So any viable strategy or tactic must be open and available to scrutiny by interested parties.

COHERENT   While the components of advanced planning can be independent of one another — and, indeed, many tactics and strategies can be standalones — a certain degree of integration should permeate all advanced planning. That is because the strategies and tactics carry within them, to varying degrees, the potential to be used for each of the four sets of advanced planning services and as such they have a bearing on each other and on the ultra-affluent client's planning as a whole. Accordingly, professional advisors should maximize any advanced planning benefits to their clients by first identifying the synergies and then accentuating their value. Even in those cases where the ultra-affluent client was not explicitly looking for results beyond a very tight mandate, a professional advisor will always work to generate optimal results and present further options.

RISK-SENSITIVE   Advanced planning runs along a scale from plain vanilla tactics and strategies at one end to the truly esoteric at the other. While everything needs to be on the proper side of the legal divide, there is clearly a lot of room to be more or less aggressive. Not surprisingly, many of the most cutting-edge, state-of-the-art strategies and tactics are more aggressive. It is therefore crucial that the ultra-affluent and their other advisors understand the level of aggressiveness and realize the pros and cons relative to each client's risk tolerance.

COST-EFFECTIVE   Given the many state-of-the-art strategies and tactics at the disposal of professional advisors, there can be instances where being on the cutting edge may carry too high a price tag for their clients. Despite the appeal of such strategies and tactics, there are nonetheless times when a more pedestrian yet cost-effective solution is sufficient. Further, there may be unforeseen complications and issues that are not apparent to less-accomplished advisors. In sum, client-centered advisors need to balance the benefits of a course of action with its costs, both financial and psychological.

COMPLEXITY-SENSITIVE   Many of the ultra-affluent want simple and readily understood solutions to their advanced planning issues. Even if the mechanics are complicated, some want a simple presentation. That way, they can make a decision quickly even though they may rely on other advisors to ultimately sign off on it. Appropriate advanced planning runs the risk of not getting implemented if the ultra-affluent client's eyes glaze over because of the level of detail. This is another example of the need to not only be able to provide expertise but to sense the most effective way to communicate that expertise on a client-by-client basis, ranging from an abecedarian overview to a highly complex flow chart. Overall, the goal of professional advisors is to learn as much about their client as possible so they can put themselves in the client's shoes and then recommend what they would do if they were in the client's position.

LEGITIMATE Needless to say, an advanced plan should never incorporate tactics or strategies that are — or that might be perceived to be — illegal or unethical. Avoiding taxes by skirting the law is necessarily out of the question. Along the same lines, with regard to wealth protection, any allegations of fraudulent transfers or any activity that will result in charges of fraud are also out of the question. Considering how much can be accomplished by staying well within the law, it is only excessive greed, ego, or sheer stupidity that results in otherwise legitimate ultra-affluent individuals crossing the line. But with so many shades of gray on the domestic front and even a broader spectrum of gray in the international arena, some very legitimate plans can seem questionable even though they are not. However, this is still a far cry from intentionally skirting the law. Ultra-affluent clients should understand that when they go deep into the gray zones, they are dramatically and ill-advisedly betting on winning the audit lottery.

THE PROFESSIONAL ADVISOR

With the Internet and television, we are all bombarded with information. For any information to be of value, however, it must be sorted through, selected, prioritized, and converted to knowledge. If you add life experience, empathy, and self-awareness to knowledge, you get wisdom. And such wisdom is the hallmark of the best professional advisors, setting them well above their competitors.

To differentiate professional advisors (in our lexicon, those who provide advanced planning services to the ultra-affluent) from other advisors, we must consider what professional advisors bring to the table as inputs and what they take away as outputs. In between is the alchemy of working with the ultra-affluent that transforms the inputs into outputs, commonly known as the Dual Star Model (Exhibit 3.4).

Exhibit 3.4

THE DUAL STAR MODEL

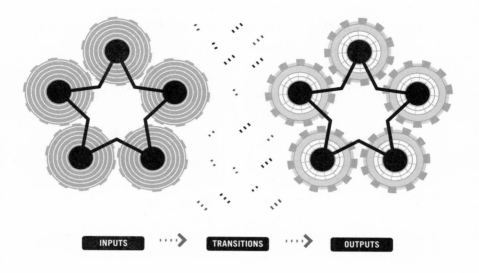

INPUTS ····> TRANSITIONS ····> OUTPUTS

INPUTS

The five inputs that professional advisors offer are:

⋱ INTERPERSONAL SKILLS To connect with the ultra-affluent, professional advisors must have exceptional interpersonal skills and they must be able to use those skills to build bridges to their wealthy clients. A bond of trust is a necessity for the professional advisor to do his or her job because intimate life details are disclosed. And, because professional advisors are usually part of an advisory team, their "people" skills must extend to their fellow advisors.

⋱ A SENSE OF PURPOSE Professional advisors have to be driven and see their providing advanced planning services as a calling. Building a successful practice with the ultra-affluent takes years — and a sense of mission. It also requires unrelenting dedication and study to achieve and maintain the necessary level of technical proficiency. And professional advisors must have the commitment and dedication to bear the oftentimes imposed role of negotiator among warring family members.

∴ CREATIVITY Creativity encompasses three elements: a knowledge of sophisticated strategies and tactics, the ability to integrate that knowledge with the goals of an ultra-affluent client to create a plan, and first-hand involvement in the development of advanced planning innovations.

∴ TECHNICAL PROFICIENCY The ultra-affluent expect the latest thinking in the areas of wealth enhancement, wealth transfer, asset protection, and charitable gifting, and they also want those tactics and strategies to be effectively implemented.

∴ INTEGRITY The very best professional advisors have a strong moral code. Their objective is to best serve their ultra-affluent clients within the confines of all applicable laws and regulations. That is why, to a degree, professional advisors select their ultra-affluent clients rather than being selected; they know which clients they can best work with.

OUTPUTS

In working with the ultra-affluent, professional advisors can come away with:

∴ FINANCIAL REWARDS It is not unheard of for a professional advisor to become one of the ultra-affluent themselves as a function of the fees and commissions that are generated by working with this wealth segment. While that is not the norm, the financial rewards of providing advanced planning services to the ultra-affluent are unquestionably significant.

∴ A REPUTATION FOR SUCCESS In enabling the ultra-affluent to realize their goals, a professional advisor builds a reputation for success, and that reputation is instrumental to the ongoing success of an advanced planning practice and likewise to landing new business.

∴ PERSONAL SATISFACTION Few professional advisors would be considered wallflowers. They tend to have strong egos and they delight in being able to flex their intellectual muscles by resolving intricate financial and legal puzzles.

∴ NEW INSIGHTS Working with the ultra-affluent is a two-way street for astute professional advisors because their relationships provide insights that can be transferred from one client to the next and also give professional advisors the grist for industry innovation.

∴ A MEANINGFUL LIFE Because the financial rewards are so significant, and because they can only effectively work with a limited number of clients at a time, professional advisors are able to create meaningful personal lives for themselves.

ADVANCED PLANNING COMPARED TO DISCRETIONARY INVESTMENT MANAGEMENT

In our experience, we have found that some advisors confuse advanced planning with discretionary investment management. The two could not be more different (Exhibit 3.5). Those who make this error tend to be relatively unsophisticated and lack an understanding of what underscores advanced planning as opposed to discretionary investment management. Very often, people who confuse the two are relatively new to the field or have not been exposed to advanced planning.

In terms of the breadth of interaction between client and advisor, discretionary investment management is consistent with advanced planning, though it does not require the same level of detail as advanced planning. The ultra-affluent are able to evaluate advice on an ongoing basis in discretionary investment management, and they also have the ability to value the services of an investment advisor on an ongoing basis. Perhaps one of the most important points of difference is that in discretionary investment management the ultra-affluent tend to retain several different advisors and remain on the lookout for other top performers to add to their stable. A strict focus on the future is also a cornerstone of discretionary investment management.

In the case of advanced planning, the breadth of interaction between client and advisor is much more situationally determined. That is, it is based on the specific needs and wants of the ultra-affluent client at a given point in time. A greater level of detail, as noted, is often essential to understanding the whole picture. The ultra-affluent are not able to evaluate advice on an ongoing basis in advanced planning. Instead their ability to evaluate is selectively limited. In advanced planning, the ability of the ultra-affluent to value the services of a professional advisor is also situationally determined. One of the most important points of difference is that in advanced planning ultra-affluent clients tend to retain just one or at most two professional advisors and they look for other professional advisors or providers on a highly selective and restrictive basis.

Exhibit 3.5

COMPARISON BETWEEN ADVANCED PLANNING AND DISCRETIONARY INVESTMENT MANAGEMENT

FACTORS	DISCRETIONARY INVESTMENT MANAGEMENT	ADVANCED PLANNING
Breadth of Interaction	Consistent	Situationally determined
Depth of Interaction	Not a requirement	Often essential
Evaluation of Advice	Ongoing	Selectively limited
Ability of a Client to Value	High	Situationally determined
Advisors Employed	Several	One or two
Focus	Future	Present and future
Scanning of Providers	Regularly	Selectively

SUMMARY

Advanced planning is the process through which advisors meet the most essential needs, wants, and demands of the ultra-affluent. In this way, advanced planning should be conceptualized as a set of services, as a methodology for applying these services, and as a way of creating exclusivity for the advisor with each and every client.

Advanced planning is the essential task of professional advisors who work with the ultra-affluent. Not to be confused with discretionary investment management, advanced planning is the way astute advisors know a client's goals are being met. Advanced planning is the process through which the advisor and the ultra-affluent ensure that they are on the same page, creating the foundation for a long-term, mutually profitable, and exclusive relationship. This exclusivity is the key to profitability for advisors to the ultra-affluent.

Chapter 4

THE VIRTUOUS CYCLE

The Virtuous Cycle is at the heart
of the advanced planning process,
guiding the professional advisor
through the fact-finding phase,
scenario thinking, the formation
and utilization of a team of advisory
specialists, the creation of an action
plan, implementation, and, finally,
any updates, reviews, or amendments to a client's plan.

ONE CAN STATE, WITHOUT EXAGGERATION,

THAT THE OBSERVATION OF AND THE SEARCH

FOR SIMILARITIES AND DIFFERENCES

ARE THE BASIS OF ALL HUMAN KNOWLEDGE.

Alfred Nobel

When working with ultra-affluent clients, professional advisors would benefit from a comprehensive yet flexible planning process, particularly one that incorporates the latest industry knowledge. The Virtuous Cycle is such a process.

The Virtuous Cycle is an alchemic process through which professional advisors can best employ their wisdom to identify solutions to client problems and develop strategies to resolve those issues. Importantly, it also addresses the ultra-affluent's apprehension about overly complex processes because it incorporates the Whole Client Model™, which increases intimacy, disclosure, and trust between clients and advisors.

Operationally, the Virtuous Cycle is composed of seven phases and contains three integrated feedback loops (Exhibit 4.1). However, while we can identify distinct phases and specific feedback loops, the ultra-affluent are not easily pigeonholed and processed; they have different needs and disparate ideas of the best way to work with advisors. Similarly, professional advisors have signature styles that have proven successful for them over the years. So the Virtuous Cycle should not be perceived as a strictly observed, immutable process, but rather as a broad conceptual model that professional advisors can interpret and adapt to their skills and to their clients' personalities.

Exhibit 4.1 |

THE VIRTUOUS CYCLE

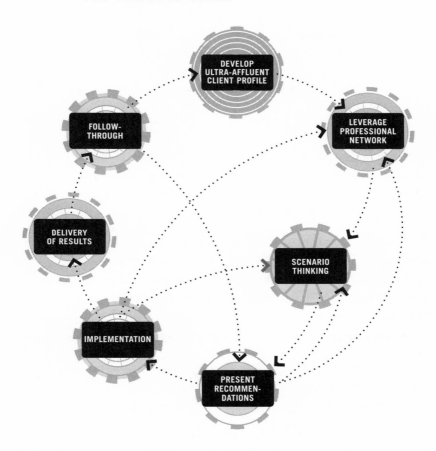

A TEAM CONCEPT

During every phase of the Virtuous Cycle, the ultra-affluent client's other advisors may be, and usually are, part of the team. The extent to which they are included is a function of the ultra-affluent client's preferences, the ways the other advisors prefer to work, and the professional advisor's own operational style.

Most ultra-affluent clients are dependent on their advisors because they readily recognize the limitations in their own expertise. Having other advisors also allows them to run the recommendations of one advisor by other members of the team. The goal is not to spur competition but to hear various points of view so the client can make better and more informed decisions. If professional advisors fail to include their fellow advisors, they run the risk of seeing their recommendations second-guessed and possibly discarded, resulting in a greater and generally wasteful expenditure of time and money, and, possibly, the loss of the ultra-affluent client.

THE BENEFITS OF FEEDBACK

Although there are specific points in the Virtuous Cycle when soliciting client feedback is the objective, professional advisors know that there are no constraints or time limits on feedback; ultra-affluent clients should always be encouraged to offer an opinion, ask a question, or share an idea. Indeed, proactively soliciting such feedback formally or informally is a key capability of top advisors regardless of their field of expertise.

Constantly seeking feedback also sets an important precedent for the give-and-take between professional advisors and their ultra-affluent clients. In such an environment, the advisor is better able to suggest tentative strategic and tactical solutions and see how the client reacts. In fact, professional advisors should frequently use trial balloons to test ideas and concepts with the ultra-affluent and then solicit feedback to help facilitate client buy-in at a later date.

It should also be understood that the ultra-affluent client can exit during any phase of the Virtuous Cycle (or, indeed, of any planning process) and, at worst, change professional advisors. However, one of the chief advantages of the Virtuous Cycle is that the risk of ultra-affluent client exits is minimized. There is such a high level of personal and professional attention built into the Virtuous Cycle that it improves the likelihood of an advisor meeting the client's expectations and not only staying on the job, but also getting more work or, in certain circumstances, referrals.

WHY THE VIRTUOUS CYCLE IS DIFFERENT

Finally, it should be noted that there is a full menu of names for client planning processes, including the Cycle of Operations, the 4-Quadrant Planning Paradigm^{SM}, and Financial Framework IV™. What differentiates the Virtuous Cycle is the way that it draws upon research and analysis. Most other models of the planning process are derived exclusively from limited advisor experience. In the development of such models, the personal experiences or techniques of one or several "top" advisors are studied and serve as models for other advisors. By contrast, the Virtuous Cycle was developed both in the trenches and in the statistical laboratory, and it encompasses years of quantitative analysis of the behaviors that elite advisors employ with the very wealthy. In this way it can be compared to the best-in-class models derived in any industry as a result of bench-marking and quality process analysis. The Virtuous Cycle has also been validated through literally thousands of structured interviews.

DEVELOPMENT OF THE
ULTRA-AFFLUENT CLIENT PROFILE

"Nothing happens without a customer" is a mantra of business school professors. In our corner of the financial services and legal industry, we would say, "Nothing happens for a professional advisor without an ultra-affluent client." And in order for professional advisors to profitably apply their skills, they require a deep understanding of the ultra-affluent clients they are working with, even when the business orientation is transactional.

Why is a deep understanding required if the professional advisor's role is to facilitate a single transaction? In a preceding chapter, we talked about an ultra-affluent client's comfort (and discomfort) level with risk and complexity. These two core elements of advanced planning alone require professional advisors to have a fairly deep understanding of the ultra-affluent clients they are working with.

The level of a professional advisor's understanding is, in turn, a function of the depth and breadth of each advisor's business model. In general, however, the more the professional advisor is being looked to for help, the higher the level of intimacy.

In every case, the professional advisor needs to create an ultra-affluent client profile. The profile is composed of the array of individual client needs, wants, facts, figures, attitudes, perceptions, preferences, social dynamics, high-net-worth personality, and thought processes. For the purposes of the Virtuous Cycle, the profile also includes insights into the personality aspects of the particular ultra-affluent client.

A NEW WAY TO FIND FACTS

We drew on the expertise of exceptionally successful professional advisors across the country, a wide variety of other skilled advisors, and research with clients to create a more refined way of profiling the affluent. In this industry there are about as many fact-finders as there are advisors to the affluent. Financial institutions, law firms, and advisors generate a whole range of fact-finding models that are, over time, customized and made a part of an advisor's own process.

Taking a close look at most fact-finders used with the wealthy, we see they tend to be skewed by their narrow focus on the assets and financials of the ultra-affluent client. Such assessments offer exhaustive detail about the client's various classes of assets, from deferred compensation to stock options. Most of these assessments do not, however, address the very aspects of the ultra-affluent client situation that will affect any and all of the solutions that a professional advisor might propose.

To create a more accurate and actionable fact-finder, we distilled the components of the client profile into six categories referred to as the Whole Client Model™. Notice that only one of the six categories is "assets" and the other five are rarely if ever included in typical fact-finders. But they should be because the ultra-affluent client's goals, their relationships, and their way of working with advisors, for example, all influence the nature and success of the client/advisor relationship.

In the Whole Client Model™, the information professional advisors require is organized into a six-sector framework that follows, along with sample questions:

GOALS

⁘ What are the client's personal and professional goals?

⁘ What does the client want or feel obligated to do for children, for other family members, for friends, for society, and for the world at large?

RELATIONSHIPS

⁘ What family member relationships (spouse, children, siblings, parents, etc.) are the most important ones in the client's personal and professional life?

⁘ What is the client's religious orientation (and how devout is he or she)?

ASSETS

⁘ How are the assets structured?

⁘ How does the client make money today (and how is that likely to change in the next three years)?

ADVISORS

⁘ Who are the other advisors the client is using and what role does each advisor play?

⁘ Of late, how frequently has the client switched selected advisors?

PROCESS

⁘ How many contacts are optimal for the client?

⁘ What security measures are they using to protect their personal and financial information?

INTERESTS

:: What are the client's favorite activities, TV programs, movies, and sport teams?

:: Are health and fitness important to the client (and, if so, what is their regimen)?

CONVERSATION NOT INTERROGATION

The majority of the details that fill each category are drawn from the ultra-affluent clients themselves. There are many approaches professional advisors can take to elaborate on and fill in each category, and they all begin with questions. Some advisors may feel that asking clients such questions is intrusive or even offensive, but we vehemently disagree. In fact, the greater majority of wealthy clients are quite willing to talk about themselves because they understand that it informs the advisor's approach to their unique situation. Furthermore, every advisor can and should be able to get the information without handing the affluent client a questionnaire or reading the questions from a fact-finder. Advisors should be able to educe the information (over the course of time, if necessary) by engaging their ultra-affluent clients in discussions about themselves, their needs, and their interests. Discreet note-taking is appropriate, but the meeting (or meetings) should take the form of a conversation, not an interrogation.

Professional advisors are adept at soliciting information from the ultra-affluent, and, not surprisingly, adroit questioning is the key to their success. Here are some of the ways those questions are categorized along with tips for eliciting information:

:: **Questions to obtain information.** The goals here are to jog the client's memory and motivate them to share.

:: **Questions that test comprehension.** In many situations, when working with an ultra-affluent client, the professional advisor needs to be certain the client is making an informed decision. It is therefore imperative that the client fully understands the issues, the alternatives, and the implications of any decision. Questions that result in client rephrasing, interpreting, comparing, and detailing accomplish this objective.

∷ **Questions that require analysis and evaluation.** Rarely are client issues cut and dry. On the contrary, they are often psychological and subtle. They involve trade-offs and issues at the core of the client's being, and they are very sensitive. Hence, the professional advisor must tactfully help the ultra-affluent client to analyze the situation or issue or consequence.

∷ **Questions that move the process forward.** When it comes to generating momentum, there is considerably more value in the adroit use of questions as opposed to assertions because questions enable the professional advisor to take the ultra-affluent client on a guided tour of self-discovery.

GROUP DYNAMICS

While questions are central to creating the profile, the context of the questions varies on a case-by-case basis. In some situations, it will be one-on-one between the professional advisor and the ultra-affluent client. At other times, the information will be solicited in a group environment with the client attended by their spouse, other family members, or one or more advisors. To manage such situations, the professional advisor must be finely attuned to group dynamics.

One way to work with an extended ultra-affluent familial unit is by facilitating an offsite meeting. The rationale for the offsite is to have key members of the family unit available to identify important issues, goals, and objectives. Experience demonstrates that offsites can be very powerful and that they can move the profiling process along expeditiously. They also provide a microcosm for observing group dynamics that may later impact other phases of the Virtuous Cycle, particularly the design of an advanced plan and its implementation.

However, while the offsite can be very effective, there are potential pitfalls that can derail the entire Virtuous Cycle. The group dynamics can be such that an open forum of ideas and preferences will be not only ineffectual but actually trigger conflict. As a result, an offsite can turn into a group therapy session where even the most astute professional advisor is out of his or her depth. Moreover, the information gleaned from the offsite may all be superficial. In sum, offsites can be valuable, but the professional advisor needs to know when and how to best employ this approach to profiling.

THE PROFESSIONAL NETWORK

With a client profile in hand, professional advisors will then turn to their professional network. The earlier that network can be enlisted in support of the advanced planning process, the better.

Socrates maintained that he was an extremely ignorant man. He held this position despite his great knowledge — or more precisely because of it; he knew enough to understand how much he did not know. Advisors should take this lesson to heart. No matter how vast their expertise, the increasingly complicated nature of advanced planning is such that there will be occasions when they are not fully informed on a subject. At these times, it behooves them to turn to specialists.

In particular, because of the often-complicated nature of the financial dealings and personal concerns of the ultra-affluent, there are many occasions when even highly skilled professional advisors must turn to a niche expert to supplement their expertise. Advanced planning for clients who have international holdings is a good example. If an ultra-affluent client has international business interests, the professional advisor will usually need to consult with experts who are intimately familiar with the appropriate laws and regulations in these foreign jurisdictions.

BUILDING A PROFESSIONAL NETWORK

In order to leverage a professional network, the advisor must first build it. And the participants in the network must meet the following criteria:

∵ **Specific expertise.** Possessing "unique" knowledge is the first screen in selecting a specialist. The expertise in question must also complement the knowledge and skills of the professional advisor without being redundant.

∵ **Integrity.** The highest ethical standards are indispensable in all aspects of advanced planning.

∵ **Professionalism.** In every way from responsiveness to inquiries to perpetual learning to affluent client management, the network participants must embrace professionalism.

∵ **Chemistry with the professional advisor.** For the professional advisor, there needs to be a comfort level when it comes to working with each of the network participants. All of the expert knowledge in the world is valueless if there is no rapport.

The participants in the professional network must "fill the gaps" in the skill sets and knowledge base of the professional advisor. Determining the participants of the network, in turn, is predicated on the nature of the more typical cases the professional advisor confronts with a consideration of the unusual ones. (To see how the professional network plays a meaningful role in the Innovation Process, see **Chapter 5: To the Edge**.)

When it comes to the expertise pipeline, there is a wide array of talents and knowledge to tap into. Attorneys and accountants are nearly always part of the professional network, as are life insurance professionals and actuaries. Increasingly, management consultants, family business specialists, and psychologists are also included in the specialist network. There are even a fair number of "off the beaten path" participants such as philosophers, mystics, and, in one instance that we know of, a cryptozoologist. Whatever the composition, a network that accurately reflects the interests and needs of an advisor's clientele will prove to be more than cost-effective.

KEEPING THE NETWORK INTACT

Once a high-quality network is put in place, it is up to the professional advisor to maintain and manage it through interpersonal skills and, of course, financial arrangements.

There are three types of financial arrangements that are prevalent in the advisory business. The first is fee-for-service through which the professional advisor buys — or rents — expertise on a case-by-case basis. With a retainer arrangement, the specialist is paid a monthly or annual fee so that they are available for consultations, usually by phone. Finally, some specialists are on a retainer and also get compensated by fee-for-service. In any case, each member of the network can benefit from the business opportunities generated by participation in the network. An attorney specializing in asset protection, for example, can not only support the professional advisor in working with the ultra-affluent but can also prepare the appropriate documents.

FINANCIAL ARRANGEMENTS WITH SPECIALISTS

Finally, while a well-functioning professional network is an indispensable tool for the top professional advisors, it also serves to ensure that the advisor is up on state-of-the-art developments in their industry, a prerequisite for those working with the ultra-affluent. That is why professional advisors take great pains to put together their network and make every effort to ensure it is structured to support their individual business models.

SCENARIO THINKING

With the client profile in hand and the expertise of a specialist network at the ready, what is the next step for the professional advisor? The answer begins with scenario thinking.

Simply put, scenario thinking is the process of generating alternative futures. From these possible outcomes, the most viable course is selected and then presented, in turn, to an ultra-affluent client's other advisors and then to the client. Scenario thinking not only has a role in the Virtuous Cycle, it is vital to the Innovation Process (see **Chapter 5: To the Edge**) and to the ongoing success of an advanced planning practice as a whole (see **Chapter 8: The Advanced Planning Practice**). For more details on scenario thinking, please turn to Appendix 2 on page 175.

PRESENTING THE RECOMMENDATIONS

Presenting recommendations to the client is a three-step process (Exhibit 4.2). The first step is to review the ultra-affluent client's profile. It is imperative that everyone — other advisors, the specialist network, and the client — has a common understanding of the client's goals, objectives, and issues. While soliciting feedback is an ongoing process, this is the time when that solicitation process is most intently focused and exhaustive.

Exhibit 4.2

PRESENT RECOMMENDATIONS

During the review, any meaningful digression from the core premises and assumptions derived from the information provided by the ultra-affluent client must be seen as a red flag. And when a red flag goes up, an advisor must return to the fact-finding phase and make sure that a client's situation and preferences have been accurately profiled and updated. Sometimes red flags go up because the ultra-affluent client was not initially comfortable enough to divulge certain facts that are crucial in the advanced planning process. Some examples that fit into this category include an honest assessment of the competencies of the heirs, the existence of an entirely separate and hidden family, or the disclosure of large pools of assets not previously mentioned.

PRESENTING THE SCENARIOS

If the client profile is confirmed as accurate, an advisor can proceed to a discussion of scenarios. At this point in the process, it is quite important to be attentive to the manner in which the ultra-affluent prefer to obtain and work with information. Some people prefer a mathematically detailed plan of action replete with diagrams and ledgers. Other ultra-affluent clients prefer to listen instead of read, and they may not even look at written material. Some prefer a highly informal, back-of-the-napkin approach, while others expect their advisor to come into the meeting with a mountain of extensive documentation.

It follows, therefore, that an advisor has to be sensitive to how to present scenarios to each ultra-affluent client. It is a best practice in this area for the professional advisor to be able to quickly switch modalities when necessary. Of course, this requires a great deal more effort and preparation, but such heavy lifting is often handsomely rewarded.

Professional advisors must be as proactive in soliciting feedback during this step as in the previous one so that any changes to the advanced plan can be expeditiously made. The nature and tone of the feedback will also provide concrete insights into the ways that the professional advisor should communicate with the ultra-affluent client.

PRESENTING THE ACTION PLAN

The ultra-affluent client is now ready to make decisions, the most important of which are whether to implement a scenario (or some of its components) or send their advisors back to the drawing board.

Keep in mind that throughout the Virtuous Cycle, ultra-affluent clients may exit if their expectations are not being met. However, the risk of this happening is diminished as long as the steps of the Virtuous Cycle are rigorously followed, and the highly interactive nature of the process usually increases the client's appreciation of the advisor's expertise as the Cycle advances toward implementation.

IMPLEMENTATION

The most familiar part of the Virtuous Cycle is implementation. Some professional advisors equate it to the time- and emotionally-intensive build-up to a wedding — after all the time and effort, it is over in a matter of hours.

The reason implementation is — or should be — so straightforward is that by this point all the hurdles have been identified and the approaches to surmounting them have been specified. That does not mean implementation is easy — in many cases, it calls for a tremendous amount of work. However, it is familiar ground to professional advisors and it is something all top advisors do extremely well. And, in the end, the key skill sets in implementation are persistence and precision, not the more-draining intuition and analysis.

Take for example, the need to obtain life insurance as part of the advanced plan. All the decisions concerning what type, how much, and how it should be structured have already been made. The next step is a matter of facilitating the underwriting process. This can take many forms, from working with the underwriting department of an insurance company to creating a new life insurance product in conjunction with a reinsurance company. It also means attending to all the other tasks involved with obtaining the policy, including the physical assessment. But, unlike the earlier phase of the Virtuous Cycle when goals are discussed and strategies weighed, it is a mechanical rather than emotional process, and it is therefore less stressful to the client and the advisor both. Further, because the client and advisor have interacted throughout the profiling, scenario, and planning stages, there is a level of trust that makes implementation easier.

A GRINDING HALT

Even so, there are changes that can derail the advanced planning process and make implementation inappropriate. Such changes, a new tax law for example, are analogous to either the bride and groom going AWOL at that grand wedding because they bring the proceedings — and implementation — to a grinding halt.

When the decision is made to not implement a plan, the professional advisor must gauge the right time to re-start the entire process. The advisor may have to again leverage the specialist network, develop new scenarios, present revised recommendations, and then begin implementation anew.

DELIVERY OF RESULTS

Too many advisors fail to benefit as they should from this phase of the process because they approach the delivery of the results in an almost perfunctory fashion. They perceive the handing over of documents and the review of what occurred in the implementation phase to be almost an afterthought.

On the contrary, the delivery of results is a critical point in the Virtuous Cycle because it sets the stage for follow-through which will, in turn and in time, generate new business for the professional advisor as the Cycle repeats itself. This is where the advisor ties the ultra-affluent client's expectations to the realities of the advanced plan. The advisor needs to take this opportunity to:

∴ **Re-confirm the ultra-affluent client profile.** Once again, it is crucial to ensure that the information upon which the advanced plan was developed and implemented is accurate. From the client's perspective, this is an ideal time for the advisor to reinforce the way that the advanced planning process has been customized to address their specific needs.

∴ **Connect the advanced plan to desired results.** Is the client getting what he or she expects and is paying for? This is the time to make sure that the advanced plan meets the client's goals.

∴ **Revise the action plan as appropriate.** As implementation is incremental, there are regular opportunities to create forward momentum concerning other components of the advanced plan.

∴ **Deepen rapport with the ultra-affluent client.** Recognizing that the ultra-affluent client is usually very receptive at this point sets the stage for the advisor to expand the depth and breadth of the relationship.

FOLLOW-THROUGH

Empirical studies conducted over more than a dozen years consistently show that advisors, even top advisors, often make a critical mistake in the period right after implementation. When asked, ultra-affluent clients feel that advisors, in general, do a less than stellar job of following through. Many advisors tend to move on to new clients, feeling that they have already made their money, and they may misperceive client feelings. Since most wealthy clients do not complain, advisors generally — and mistakenly — conclude that those clients are satisfied.

Follow-through is crucial because it makes the ultra-affluent client feel attended to, and, as we have seen, attention is a vital component and driving expectation for such clients. Not only is this the ethical course of action, it is also central to building a sustainable and successful advanced planning practice. Follow-through comes in three forms: the focused applications of the innovation process, ultra-affluent or advisor driven contact, and periodic reviews.

FOCUSED APPLICATIONS OF THE INNOVATION PROCESS
The ultra-affluent client profile is in the data-management system of the professional advisor. So, as the innovation process proceeds — as new strategies and/or tactics are developed and validated — the

advisor is well positioned to bring selected strategies and tactics to those clients who would most benefit from them.

From time to time there is also the necessity for a more formal updating of the ultra-affluent client profile. The recommendation of a new strategy or tactic is predicated on the accuracy of the client profile so, as client circumstances frequently change, regular updating of the client profile will enable the advisor to evaluate whether a given advanced planning strategy or tactic fits with the client's risk- and complexity-tolerance.

ULTRA-AFFLUENT CLIENT AND/OR ADVISOR DRIVEN CONTACT
There are many times when the ultra-affluent client and/or that client's other advisors will reestablish contact with the professional advisor because of changes in circumstances. Anything that impacts the agenda of the client such as marriages, births, and deaths should prompt a reconnection with the professional advisor. When this occurs, there is a need to update the client profile and then proceed through the various phases of the Virtuous Cycle once again.

If the client directly contacts the professional advisor, circumventing other members of the advisory team, it behooves the advisor to bring the other advisors into the loop. A quick phone call is a wonderful way to head off any hurt feelings or bad blood.

PERIODIC REVIEWS Due to the nature of advanced planning, it is a given that the professional advisor will need to intermittently meet with the ultra-affluent client and the client's other advisors to ensure everything is going in the right direction, that all the moving parts of a strategy or tactic are working in concert. While an annual review is the norm in the investment management field, advanced planning reviews should not be governed by the calendar but by the strategy or tactic employed and by the client's preferences.

Depending on the familiarity and proficiency of the other advisors, it is often useful for the professional advisor to meet with them first and make sure that the members of the advisory team are on the same page.

REMEMBERING THE HUMAN ELEMENT

While advanced planning can employ some of the most sophisticated thinking in the financial services arena, it is a mistake to place too much emphasis on the technical wizardry involved. As opposed to what game theory would tell us, human dynamics are more important to the advanced planning process than technical know-how.

Though most advisors would second the notion that their interpersonal skills are more valuable in building relationships than their industry knowledge, they regularly behave otherwise. All too often, the human side is subsidiary to financial, technical, and legal expertise. If the Virtuous Cycle is to succeed, however, professional advisors must be acutely attuned to the emotional side of their ultra-affluent clients. Advanced planning obliges those clients to consider the intimate details of their lives, and such scrutiny can be discomfiting. Clients will need a lot of help and support to move from conflict or ambivalence to a recognition of opportunities and potentials, and it is the advisor's job to expedite that transition.

SUMMARY

The Virtuous Cycle is the process whereby the best professional advisors strive to best serve their ultra-affluent clients. The Virtuous Cycle structures the interaction between the professional advisor and the ultra-affluent client. It also creates a set of ethical processes for serving the needs of the ultra-affluent while ensuring that the client's needs and interests are optimized at all times. If ultra-affluent clients respond positively to the Cycle, it helps professional advisors grow their businesses.

At the operational level, the Virtuous Cycle consists of phases that a professional advisor steers an ultra-affluent client through, beginning with profiling and fact-finding and ending with the implementation of the advanced plan. However, in the hands of experienced professional advisors, the Virtuous Cycle never stops because it accommodates constantly changing client needs and circumstances. Advanced planning is not static; it is dynamic and ongoing.

As we have seen, the Virtuous Cycle is composed of seven phases and it contains three integrated feedback loops. Although these phases and feedback loops are depicted in the model, that is merely a depiction of the ideal; only rarely does an ultra-affluent client go through the process phase by phase from start to finish. Rather, the Cycle is a conceptual model or a roadmap to guide professional advisors who understand that they will occasionally have to take detours or backtrack to meet the changing needs of their ultra-affluent clients.

Part | III

AT THE
CUTTING EDGE

To best serve their clients and
distinguish themselves in a crowded
and highly competitive field,
professional advisors have to keep
up with the state of their industry —
with the strategies, tactics, and
products that are being developed
— and know whether those new
solutions are suitable for their
clients. In the effort to stand out
from the crowd, however, advisors
should never lose sight of what
is legal and what is right.

Chapter 5

TO THE EDGE

To thrive in the ultra-affluent
marketplace, professional advisors
must differentiate themselves from
their competitors. And the power
of differentiation, however
ephemeral, lies with those who
can best marshal information and
use their imagination to envision
new, customized client solutions.

IMAGINATION IS MORE IMPORTANT THAN KNOWLEDGE.

Albert Einstein

The stratosphere of private wealth is populated by the ultra-affluent. In this rarified atmosphere, there are distinct needs and wants that can't be addressed by the solutions developed for the less financially endowed. In order to work at these fiscal heights, professional advisors must bring more to the table than proficiency with commodity-like products; they must be standing at the cutting edge and offer their ultra-affluent clients state-of-the-art thinking and precision execution. They must prove their worth — and their superiority to their fellow advisors — through their uniqueness. They must differentiate and brand themselves within the ultra-affluent marketplace.

Some advisors try to differentiate themselves by offering one-stop shopping for the full slate of financial solutions. Others profess to be experts in a particular area such as estate or charitable planning, and still others hang their hat on their accomplishments as experts in one or more transactions. In short, advisors with a specific area of competence can give their clients a reason why they should be selected as the advisor of choice.

Selecting and working on such an area of focus in order to achieve competitive differentiation is vital. Clients are approached by legions of advisors seeking their business and they need a compelling reason to favor one over another. Even so, maintaining a point of differentiation within a service industry can be exceedingly difficult because the differentiation of any service is, by definition, relatively easy to replicate.

Consider the case of a retail bank. The bank decides to compete on a new front — to differentiate itself — by opening branches in supermarkets. When customers respond positively, other banks will follow the leader and possibly improve upon the original idea. The same would happen to an insurance company that develops a cutting-edge product; if it works, the competition will follow suit. So when it comes to advisors who work at this level of wealth, the best they can hope for is "de facto uniqueness."

DE FACTO UNIQUENESS

We refer to cutting-edge strategies and tactics as "de facto uniqueness" because there is no true uniqueness in the financial services universe. Unique (as in differentiated) services are too easy to replicate. There is no way to patent or to defend a patent of a cutting-edge strategy in financial services. Still, these strategies and tactics are unique for a time because they are developed on a customized basis for an individual client. They are also unique to the degree that only a relative handful of advisors can comprehend them, let alone implement them, and even fewer are capable of providing the appropriate ongoing support and servicing.

These strategies and tactics are also unique because those professional advisors working successfully with the ultra-affluent are always striving to better understand the laws and regulations. By carefully pushing against the edge of what is currently "accepted practice," professional advisors are able to detect ways to leverage cutting-edge strategies and tactics on behalf of their clients. Implementing a solution for one's clients and then finding other opportunities results in cascading first-mover advantages. By persistently working at the ultra-affluent level and by doggedly pursuing differentiation, professional advisors can brand themselves in the very crowded advisory market even when the point of differentiation is replicated because they will be perceived as the groundbreakers and innovators (for more, see **Chapter 7: Evaluating the Opportunity**).

As we have seen, advanced planning for the ultra-affluent is about bringing to bear specific expertise that enables clients to fulfill their financial agenda. In this sense, that expertise is defined as a grounding in skills and insights that are a product of experience and sophisticated knowledge. Additionally, that expertise is embodied by the ability to move to the cutting edge in thinking and action without taking that misstep over the edge. The way professional advisors are able to perpetually stay state of the art and on the edge is through the application of the Innovation Process.

THE INNOVATION PROCESS

The Innovation Process is the cerebral side of success in an advanced planning practice. It is where the brain power of professional advisors and their professional network moves the industry forward through highly creative thinking. It is where they tip the scales of success by differentiating themselves in meaningful ways. It is where the ultra-affluent clients are able to succeed financially in ways that would today seem improbable or impossible.

The Innovation Process starts with evaluating where we are today and concludes with a viable strategy or tactic specifically suited to the ultra-affluent. The process is in many ways a search for nuance. It is often a matter of identifying a wrinkle in the tax code and knowing under what conditions the ultra-affluent can benefit. As such, the Innovation Process is often about developing processes and systems that can turn a breakthrough idea into a viable strategy or tactic or even a new product.

The Innovation Process is composed of four interconnected processes that can ensure state-of-the-art results (Exhibit 5.1). They are: 1) environmental scanning, keeping a weather eye out for new and emerging industry trends; 2) scenario thinking, envisioning where those trends might lead under certain situations; 3) actualization, turning hypothetical ideas into real strategies, tactics, and products; and 4) validation, implementing and regularly updating the innovation.

Exhibit 5.1

THE INNOVATION PROCESS

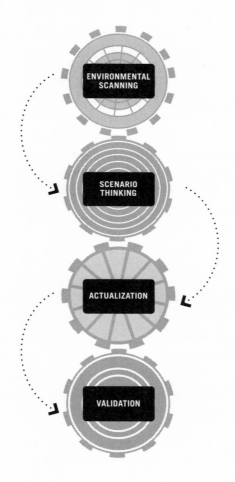

Because the Innovation Process is quite fluid it can be hard to capture. It is easier to understand if we consider each of its component processes as distinct. After we explore each of the four component processes, we will demonstrate the Process by applying the framework to one of today's hottest venues for new strategies, tactics, and products — private placement variable life insurance.

ENVIRONMENTAL SCANNING

Environmental scanning is at the core of the Innovation Process. Professional advisors are perpetually engaging in environmental scanning in order to be aware of the evolving legal and regulatory landscape as well as the changing preferences and requirements of the ultra-affluent.

Environmental scanning is a three-part discipline. The first part entails keeping abreast of legal and regulatory situations, and questions that the professional advisor should constantly be asking include:

∷ How are the tax laws changing in various jurisdictions?

∷ What effect will the changes have on the ultra-affluent?

∷ Which tax court cases, IRS memoranda, regulations, and private letter rulings are opening avenues that need to be considered?

The second part is the constant evaluation of the competitive landscape. In this context, professional advisors are perpetually appraising the strategies, tactics, and products that appear on their radar screens. They need to be acutely aware of what is out there. This knowledge has the side benefit of helping them to devise ever more sophisticated iterations of any new strategies, tactics, and products that would be expressly suited to their ultra-affluent clientele.

The third part involves the ongoing assessment of the needs, wants, and preferences of the ultra-affluent as both a single and a highly segmented market. For the purposes of the Innovation Process, certain types of segmentation schemes are especially effective, including:

∷ Psychographics (see **Chapter 2: The Ultra-Affluent**);

∷ Levels of wealth (see **Chapter 1: Varieties of Affluence**); and

∷ The nature and source of their assets.

Of course, successful professional advisors already undertake environmental scanning. The problem is that environmental scanning can often be unconscious or reflexive as opposed to systematic and rigorous. As a result, nuances can be overlooked and competitive advantages can be forfeited.

A TICKET TO SUCCESS

Over time, we have empirically concluded that those professional advisors who are most systematic at environmental scanning are the ones best positioned to succeed. Professional advisors who period- ically examine trends with their colleagues, with members of their network, and with wealthy clients have an advantage over their competitors. Professional advisors who use the occasion of a market or business planning process to look at environmental trends are more successful. So, in a highly competitive industry where differentiation is key, it behooves professional advisors to put in place the systems and structures that will enable them to collect and distill the types of information that will create this important competitive advantage.

There are many different ways to scan the environment. All of them have certain potential utility and each has some value. For instance, high-end industry conferences were once a prime place to get a state- of-the-industry update and tap into trends. Increasingly, however, because the industry is so competitive, the top thinkers and innovators have no incentive to share their thinking (unless, of course, they are looking for split business or are wholesaling). Trade publica- tions have become barren ground for new ideas for the same reason.

WHERE ARE ALL THE NEW IDEAS?

So where should an advisor search for new ideas? As we saw in Chapter 4, personal and professional relationships are the ideal support system for personal and professional advantage, and one of the best primary sources for new ideas is fellow advisors who can be trusted. They could be part of a professional advisor's support network or an expert study group. In fact, with the shutting down of other communication channels for state-of-the-art thinking, study groups — a mainstay among many professional advisors — have taken on even greater significance.

In any event, being proactive is the only way to stay on top of the current competitive environment, and environmental scanning should always be considered when talking with other advisors, when reading, or when dealing with ultra-affluent clients.

Our recommendation is to formalize this process by carefully thinking through the mechanisms to collect the appropriate data and developing databases to effectively manage all the facts, opinions, and ideas that are collected. Of course, just getting and storing the data is not enough. It has to be converted into information on which to base business decisions, and to take that step, the raw material of environmental scanning must be transformed into scenarios that can drive business decision making.

SCENARIO THINKING

After information is collected through environmental scanning, a professional advisor, often supported by a professional network, should next engage in scenario thinking (for more on scenario thinking, see **Appendix 2** on page 175).

Scenarios are hypothetical futures that an advisor or an ultra-affluent client might encounter, and each scenario has a probability and a risk assessment associated with it. For example, a scenario of a prolonged bear market and worldwide economic recession might have a medium-to-low probability of occurring but a high risk factor in the event that it did occur.

When applied to the Innovation Process, scenario thinking is used to develop a number of potentially viable strategies and tactics. By looking at the scenarios that are most probable, it is possible to create business strategies that will not only reduce business risk but increase the likelihood of success. Scenario thinking can also lead indirectly to a new financial product or service.

Like environmental scanning, scenario thinking is an almost continuous endeavor, and the top professional advisors are constantly thinking of new ways to serve their ultra-affluent clients. One of the best arguments for making scenario thinking an ongoing discipline is the simple fact that innovative ideas can come from anywhere at anytime. Science is full of stories of serendipitous discoveries. Take the case of the discovery of the carbon-based benzene ring, a fundamental concept of organic chemistry. After many hours of trying to puzzle out the structure of this molecule, Friedrich Kekule fell asleep while watching the dance of flames in a fire. He dreamed of a snake that coiled and coiled around before eventually swallowing its own tail and awoke to understand intuitively how carbon atoms are organized in benzene and how that organization is related to the special properties of benzene. Science is full of stories of discovery based on hard work combined with intuition. So is the field of financial advisory services; we repeatedly hear professional advisors recount the serendipitous ways they arrived at their creative concepts.

A CREATIVE ENDEAVOR

In this extremely competitive environment, being able to develop an executable strategy or tactic is a highly creative endeavor. It is necessary for a professional advisor to not only see the possibilities, but to be able to transform those possibilities into probabilities. To do that, professional advisors need to marry their considerable interpersonal expertise with technical expertise. There are plenty of good examples to emulate. High-end life insurance professionals, for instance, were the "creators" of the modern fund-of-funds business, as well as the ESOP. Some have even taken the work of the Wall Street derivative gurus and done them one better.

In the context of the Innovation Process, we can drill down and separate all the distinct sub-processes. In this way, we can clarify the thinking patterns that are most likely to produce viable strategies, tactics, and products for the ultra-affluent. The thinking patterns described here are related to conceptual disciplines in other fields, such as Janusaian thinking, the synthesthia of intelligences, processing through selective encoding, combinatorial analyses, and integrated comparisons.

In any case, scenario thinking leads to new strategies and tactics, ideas that look good on the drawing board. The next step of the Innovation Process is to bring those strategies and tactics to life for ultra-affluent clients.

ACTUALIZATION

For a new strategy, tactic, or product to work, it needs to be actionable. "Delivering the best service" is a laudable goal, but it is not actionable. "Delivering excellent service by creating a six-month agenda of actions with a client and following up regularly" is a precise and actionable goal. In sum, to move the product of scenario thinking from the drawing board to the street, it must be operationally precise.

Actualization is the process of connecting all the dots in the "real world" and making certain the strategy, tactic, or product is all it appears to be. Everything that is required to make the idea work effectively is delineated and put in place. Often, the first step in actualization is enlisting key resources. Most professional advisory firms do not have the internal resources to actualize a new way of doing business and must rely on outside help, so the experts who can be outsourced should be delineated and evaluated. For advanced planning, the pool of experts includes:

∷ Senior executives at insurance companies

∷ Managing directors at trust companies

∷ Derivative specialists

∷ Actuaries

∷ Appraisers

∷ Legal experts

- Accountants
- Tax specialists
- Psychologists and/or sociologists

THE ROLE OF TECHNOLOGY

Very often, a central component of actualization is technological support. There are two aspects to this. One aspect of actualization through technology involves the software needed to conduct ultra-affluent client analyses with modeling and presentation capabilities. Sometimes, existing software with some modification is more than sufficient to meet this need. On other occasions, entirely new software models must be constructed.

The other technological aspect of actualization is the ability to deliver value to the client on an ongoing basis. This requires product or service administration and management. Again, some of these strategies and tactics will require the development of new software, while others will not.

THE ROLE OF TECHNOLOGY IN ACTUALIZATION

While scenario thinking can result in excellent ideas for ultra-affluent clients, the cost of implementation is often an obstacle. In order to determine feasibility, a cost-benefit calculation is a useful technique. Simulated discrete choice modeling is occasionally used when the cost of designing and developing a strategy, tactic, or product is high.

VALIDATION

Even when scenario thinking works wonderfully well on paper and the supporting expert and technological mechanisms and structures are in place, questions remain. Will it really work with current clients? Will it appeal to new clients? Will it grow the business? To answer these questions, the professional advisor must take an idea to market to validate its worth.

Besides the questions in the paragraph above, other issues now need to be addressed. Validation encompasses two additional considerations: one legal or regulatory and the other ethical. On the legal or regulatory front, the advisor must make certain all the concepts are vetted appropriately. Do they meet currently accepted legal and regulatory notions or do they stretch one or more current definitions? How close to the edge is the new scenario? How aggressive is the strategy or tactic? Getting too near the edge of what is currently accepted practice invites risk and risks, though not necessarily bad, often have cost and other implications.

The other consideration — ethics — is more complicated. Thinking through the ethical nature of the strategy or tactic is as important as thinking through the legal and regulatory implications. After all, just because something *can* be done does not mean it *should* be done. For example, there are ways of protecting assets after the fact and dodging the matter of fraudulent conveyance. Are these ways legal? In certain circumstances, they are. Are they ethical? Should a professional advisor employ them? Professional advisors need to distinguish between legal and ethical behavior. It is not enough for a new strategy or tactic to be legal; it must also be ethical. (For more on this issue, see **Chapter 6: Over the Edge**).

PRIVATE PLACEMENT
VARIABLE LIFE INSURANCE

All of the elements of the Innovation Process can be illustrated within the context of private placement variable life insurance. BPN Montaigne LLC has extensive experience in providing completely customized private placement variable life insurance solutions for ultra-affluent clients, and the following is derived from that experience as well as that of a small number of other professional advisors with similar expertise.

ENVIRONMENTAL SCANNING   Right now, there is tremendous interest in private placement variable life insurance because it is one of the most efficient ways to address particular needs of the ultra-affluent. Our studies of the ultra-affluent clients who have already obtained this product show that their evaluations are extremely positive. At the same time, our studies of the ultra-affluent clients who are not using this product reveal that there is tremendous interest in learning more. Our recent research also shows that there is increasing interest among the affluent for alternative investments and for investment-oriented tax management. It follows that there will be increasing interest in private placement variable life insurance.

Ultra-affluent clients like the fact that private placement variable life insurance lets them trade off paying income taxes on portfolio income and transactions for the costs inherent in private placement variable life insurance. In this way, the capital gains taxes generated by high-turnover hedge funds, for instance, can be eliminated. The fact that the assets placed in the policy can, with minor additional maneuvering, be made secure from creditors and litigants is an important side benefit.

Private placement variable life insurance is not new nor is it truly unique. However, it is now being marketing more aggressively than ever before, and, as a consequence of the marketing push, it is being used more frequently to solve the financial problems of selected wealthy clients. The financial services industry is currently taking a range of approaches to providing this product to clients. At one end of the spectrum, advisors are providing an enhanced version of conventional variable life insurance. At the other end, advisors are providing totally customized approaches adapted to their individual ultra-affluent clients. There are other variations of the product lying between the two ends of the spectrum. For the ultra-affluent, the appropriate kind of private placement variable life insurance is very much a function of the individual and the situation.

Furthermore, we have conducted several extensive studies of client reactions to private placement variable life insurance both before and after purchase. According to the research, clients respond most positively to customized policies; the ultra-affluent, in keeping with what we have already learned about them, like the idea of being unique and having products that address their uniqueness. Importantly, customization conveys to the ultra-affluent the fact that an advisor fully understands their unique persona and distinct needs. Ultra-affluent clients also like to have the chance to designate — within certain parameters — the investment managers in the private placement variable life insurance product.

A thorough review of private placement variable life insurance demonstrates how the professional advisor can scan the environment to detect an opportunity; in this case, the increasing demand for private placement variable life insurance among the ultra-affluent. Advisors were able to link the needs of their clients to products already being marketed and identify a particular role for private placement variable life insurance.

SCENARIO THINKING So far, in looking at private placement variable life insurance we have approached it as a product. That is, we have looked at its features, especially customization. But that is not the only way to look at private placement variable life insurance. By employing scenario thinking, we can examine the possibilities of meaningfully enhancing the product beyond its current basic features, and we can also identify ways to adroitly employ and apply the product in the larger context of ultra-affluent client situations.

We have seen, sometimes implemented, and occasionally marveled at some of the strategies, tactics, and products professional advisors have employed to provide private placement variable life insurance to their ultra-affluent clients. The following are examples of the benefits of some of those strategies:

∷ Obtaining a substantial tax deduction of more than 75 percent while simultaneously creating a dynasty trust benefiting grandchildren and future generations. This was done while optimizing the cost/benefit relationship and eliminating the payment of estate and gift taxes.

∷ Creating a conservation trust funded in perpetuity with half the monies coming from matching governmental and other private sources. This solution created a deferred income stream equal to the net present value of the initial investment for the benefit of heirs.

∷ Obtaining enhanced investment returns resulting in a doubling of the returns over a 20-year period with private placement variable life insurance (as opposed to not wrapping the investment). In this structure, it was possible to make certain heirs receive all the assets of the estate without paying any income or estate taxes.

∷ Facilitating a gift of art and the accompanying financial support in perpetuity. This gift enabled the benefactor to generate income for life that actuarially will be two-to-three times larger than the value donated.

∷ For investment talent, creating a nonqualified plan and funding it with their "own" investment performance.

∷ Creating a trust benefiting the grandchildren that can circumvent the need to pay estate taxes on assets of $100 million or more. In this case, the investments provide for lifetime income of $10 million or more with minimal tax obligations.

∷ Diversifying a concentrated and highly appreciated equity position without paying capital gains taxes while concurrently hedging a well diversified portfolio and generating a steady stream of tax-free revenue, all at a net zero cost.

∴ Protecting investment assets from creditors and litigants while multiplying the investment return and payout which is also protected even though the client has limited input into the advisory process.

Can all these scenarios be actualized? Yes; in fact, these are actual cases from advisors and they have passed a legal screen. However, the ethical question is whether they should be and that is another matter. Indeed, concerns about whether such solutions should be permitted may soon result in closer regulatory scrutiny. And, given the drive of advisors for differentiation, we can be sure that a plethora of additional scenarios will soon emerge, some of which may prove to be less actionable. The point is that scenario thinking should not be restrictive. When professional advisors and the super-specialists they work with engage in scenario thinking they should not censor themselves. Instead, they should "play" with the ideas because it is impossible to tell where it will all lead. Once ideas have been articulated, the riskier ones can be screened out.

ACTUALIZATION With scenarios in hand, the professional advisor must put in place the structures and systems, must ascertain preferred financial institutions, and, often, must develop financial software models to make a scenario viable. To better understand this stage, let us consider a totally customized private placement variable life insurance product.

As part of ultra-affluent client profiling (see **Chapter 5: The Virtuous Cycle**), it is imperative to determine the feasibility of the product for an individual ultra-affluent client. While there are a number of ways to do this, BPN Montaigne LLC developed a 12-point assessment tool. After the tool is scored, it provides viability guidelines and also delineates the structural requirements.

An increasing number of insurance companies are seeking to be the wrapper of choice for those professional advisors providing customized private placement variable life insurance. Therefore, it is critical to be able to evaluate the wrappers on a case-by-case basis.

To this end, BPN Montaigne LLC also developed a 42-issue product evaluator that looks at everything from structure and pricing to retention limits and reinsurance. The ability to conduct such an evaluation has proven to be key as there are a number of pitfalls that can ensnare the product, the ultra-affluent client, and, consequently the professional advisor. These pitfalls also help identify additional actualization problems.

Some of these pitfalls are across-the-board problems, some are product-structuring problems, and some occur post-sale. To get a better feel for what can go wrong and what the professional advisor must be attentive to, let us briefly consider each category of problems.

The across-the-board problems (and potential vulnerabilities) can not only negate the benefits of the private placement variable life insurance but can also cause considerable down-stream difficulties for all involved parties. A few such problems that we see on the horizon include:

- Disqualification of the product as life insurance. When this happens, all the income will be taxable as it occurs, thus eliminating the benefits associated with the life insurance wrapper.

- Requiring that money must be taken out of the policy, resulting in a taxable event. This can happen, for example, when the investment performance creates a Section 7702 corridor problem and there is not enough life insurance in reserve.

- The policy runs afoul of the modified endowment contract rules because of poor construction or because the product changes over time.

- The policy matures as an endowment or, worse still, lapses. In the case of maturity as an endowment, the gains are taxed as ordinary income. When the policy lapses, there is phantom income.

Structuring problems reflect the improper construction of the policy on the part of the advisor. This does not mean that such a policy cannot be sold; at this level of complexity, improperly structured products are sold all too often. But the policy will not work properly, with the consequence that the client may not actually receive the benefits they seek. Examples of initial structuring problems include:

∴ The ultra-affluent client's goals and qualifications are not accurately assessed. This is becoming more and more common in those cases where private placement variable life insurance is an enhanced variable product. It can also occur when private placement variable life insurance is presented as a panacea — a tax-management strategy capable of mitigating most, if not all, tax consequences. Private placement variable life insurance is a very powerful tool when used properly, but trying to make it a cure-all is a recipe for disaster.

∴ An inappropriate insurance company is selected to provide the wrapper. With the seeming attractiveness of the market, many insurance companies are creating private placement variable life products, but that does not mean they will be able to develop the right product and support system.

∴ Related to the above point, the situs for application and policy can make a very big difference to the ultra-affluent client, a fact that few insurance companies have taken into account. When considering such things as state premium taxes as well as asset protection, the situs for application and policy can have a dramatic impact. It is also an issue when the decision is made to go offshore.

Regulatory oversight and structuring problems are not the only difficulties that may emerge with this product line. Post-sale problems can arise because the policy is sold and then "forgotten." As with all financial products, there is a clear need to carefully monitor the performance of the product (and the situation of the client) and to be prepared to make adjustments when needed. Unfortunately, a growing body of anecdotal evidence suggests that most advisors today are marketing private placement variable life insurance as a one-time transaction. Post-sale problems can come from a number of sources, including:

∷ The reproposal and monitoring systems of the carrier or professional advisor are inadequate. For instance, there is limited in-force policy illustration capability or limited in-force concept (i.e., split-dollar) illustration capability.

∷ There is no or limited ongoing monitoring. Ultra-affluent client situations change, investment performance impacts the product, and policy structures are affected.

Because of the many pitfalls, there is the need to be able to run scenarios as part of the Virtuous Cycle. Because of severe deficiencies in what many of the insurance companies have developed, BPN Montaigne LLC as well as a number of other professional advisors have developed their own financial software models to augment and better manage the data provided by insurance companies. Such software takes into account the many factors that need to be considered such as:

∷ Investment return friction

∷ Alternative tax environments

∷ Investment characteristic assumptions

∷ Jurisdictional considerations

∷ Ultra-affluent client specific design considerations

VALIDATION   When it comes to private placement variable life insurance as a product, due diligence is fairly straightforward. On the legal/regulatory side, there are a number of considerations such as: "Is the product life insurance?" and "Is there investor control?" When it comes to ethical considerations, the professional advisor must weigh the risk to the ultra-affluent client as well as to the other advisors working with that client.

We previously pointed out that private placement variable life insurance is not new. As such the validation issues when looking at it as a product have been well detailed. On the other hand, when private placement variable life insurance is integrated into a sophisticated advanced planning strategy, the professional advisor must be very careful in evaluating the legal/regulatory and ethical footing for the strategy.

SUMMARY

The most skilled and successful professional advisors are relentless in their pursuit of the Innovation Process. For those professional advisors on the cutting edge, the ones who have mastered the ability to constantly compete through differentiation, innovation is a way of life. Every client interaction, every trade publication, every professional interaction is a potential source of a new, client-serving idea.

For these leading professionals, the four components that make up the Innovation Process are consciously or subconsciously at work at all times. The very best professional advisors, for example, are continually involved in environment scanning, and they are constantly conceiving and vetting new scenarios.

Through our research, we have found that the greater majority of professional advisors as well as the super-specialists they work with immerse themselves in the Innovation Process. What is the consequence of all this creative effort from the business perspective? We believe that the Innovation Process enables professional advisors to brand themselves and maintain a sustainable competitive advantage. It is sustainable because the competitive advantage is always reinventing itself. The Innovation Process can be compared to the tireless hunt for a killer application, one that will, for a period of time, eliminate the competition by allowing advisors to uniquely meet the needs and wants of the ultra-affluent.

Chapter 6

OVER THE EDGE

While aggressively looking for the latest and most effective tactics and strategies on behalf of their clients, professional advisors must be careful that they don't compromise their clients' best interests and their own careers by crossing any legal or ethical boundaries.

EXPEDIENTS ARE FOR THE HOUR,

BUT PRINCIPLES ARE FOR THE AGES.

Henry Ward Beecher

What would some people do to save $10 million or more in taxes? What would a person do to keep their wealth from the courts? As it turns out a great many wealthy individuals and their advisors will sometimes take substantial risks to maintain and enhance the clients' fortunes, even when those risks are inappropriate in every respect.

There is a great demand for services that enable taxes to be evaded, just as there is a great demand for services to protect and hide assets. At the same time, regrettably, there are many advisors who are more than willing to assist the wealthy on these fronts, especially if they are well paid.

ABUSIVE TRUSTS

Once we accept the fact that a relative handful of unscrupulous advisors and their wealthy clients will seek to bend or circumvent the law, we will shortly uncover a broad variety of approaches that range from the legal and the questionable all the way to the downright illegal. In some cases, there is no question about the illegality of what is being done — just consider that current estimates of the hundreds of millions of dollars being laundered every year, accounting for about a quarter of the money in circulation round the globe. On a far smaller but no less illegal scale, there are many ways for ultra-affluent clients to go "over the edge," including abusive trust structures.

Abusive trust schemes usually entail the creation of a number of trusts, whether domestic or offshore, to which the client assigns selected assets as well as income. The trusts are vertically layered so that each trust distributes income to the next trust. Bogus expenses are charged against the trust income, thereby reducing the taxable income (Exhibit 6.1). At the same time, the illusion of separation of control is created. Specifically, while the advisor is supposedly the trustee, the ultra-affluent client actually controls the trust.

Exhibit 6.1

LAYERING IN ABUSIVE TRUSTS

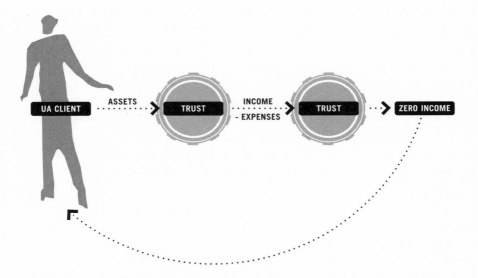

There are quite a number of abusive domestic trust arrangements, including:

∷ THE ABUSIVE ASSET MANAGEMENT COMPANY An asset management company formed as a domestic trust is created where the ultra-affluent client is the director. Meanwhile, the advisor is the trustee responsible for running the asset management company. The objective of this arrangement is for the client to convey the impression that he or she is not managing his or her businesses, thereby starting the layering process.

∷ THE ABUSIVE BUSINESS TRUST The ultra-affluent client transfers a business to a trust, receiving certificates or units of beneficial interest. The business trust makes payments to the unit holders — the client — or other trusts, so that the business trust does not have to pay any taxes. The business trust can supposedly be set up so that the units are canceled at death or sold to the owner's heirs for a nominal cost, thus avoiding estate taxes.

∴ THE ABUSIVE FAMILY RESIDENCE TRUST   The ultra-affluent client transfers his or her family residence (including furnishings) to a trust, receiving units that are claimed to be part of a taxable exchange. The exchange results in a stepped-up basis for the property. At the same time, the owner does not report a gain. The trust is thus in the rental business and claims to rent the residence back to the ultra-affluent client. However, in many instances, no rent is paid as the owner and family are identified as caretakers of the property.

∴ THE ABUSIVE FINAL TRUST   When a number of abusive trusts are being employed, some ultra-affluent clients create a final trust that holds the trust units of other abusive trusts and is the distributor of their income. Commonly, the final trust is created in a foreign jurisdiction which imposes little if any tax on the trust.

Tax laundering employing abusive trusts is a relatively new area of fraud, having only been tracked by the Criminal Investigation unit of the IRS since October 1998. Even though the vast majority of such cases probably go undetected, there was, as Exhibit 6.2 shows, an increase in the number of indictments and convictions from 1999 to 2000, a testament to the government's growing resolve to close legal loopholes.

Exhibit 6.2

CRIMINAL INVESTIGATIONS STATISTICS

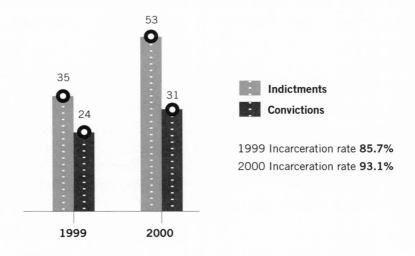

Indictments

Convictions

1999 Incarceration rate **85.7%**
2000 Incarceration rate **93.1%**

OFFSHORE TRUSTS

In spite of what many promoters say, there is no way to save income taxes using an offshore trust, and many such trusts are established solely to attenuate tax liabilities and/or shelter assets.

Too often, however, offshore trusts are over-promoted as cure-alls by advisors who do not fully understand the strict legal requirements that make the trusts work for the ultra-affluent. Some of the more common complications include forced heirship rights, direct or indirect control, and inappropriate letters of wishes.

To enhance their attractiveness, certain offshore jurisdictions have mutated the trust concept with both positive and negative results. Unfortunately, advisors often fail to recognize the potential complications. As a result, more and more offshore trusts are being scrutinized and challenged. The affluent who placed their wealth in trust a couple of generations ago are dying out and disappointed relatives, disgruntled business partners, former spouses, creditors, and litigants, as well as revenue authorities often end up launching a determined challenge.

Recent legislation has shown that trusts, including offshore trusts, can be put aside as would be the case when the settlor retains control, when the assets are located in a jurisdiction that fails to recognize the trusts, or when the trust fails to conform with essential equity criteria. Even when everything about the establishment of the trust is proper, it can still be put aside if it is being improperly administered.

OVERLY AGGRESSIVE

Moving away from the black zone of clearly illegal acts, we enter the far more complicated gray zone where the legality of a given maneuver is open to interpretation. This is the dominion where an advisor's integrity, or lack thereof, becomes readily apparent. However, simply because a professional advisor can find a "friendly" attorney to get the "right" answer as evidenced by a favorable opinion letter, it does not mean that such an opinion abrogates the relevant legal considerations, the pertinent moral issues, or, above all, the advisor's responsibility to his or her clients.

To combat the ease with which advisors could get legal opinions that supported their actions in gray areas, the Clinton administration issued rules that strengthen the ability of the IRS to police "tax shelters." The government is also cracking down on attorneys who endorse the use of advanced planning strategies as well as those who provide opinion letters to legally questionable strategies. These tougher measures will not completely discourage people who are promoting tax schemes or the ultra-affluent clients who are looking for ways to sidestep the rules. And it is not only advisors at the fringes who are intimately involved in abetting the wealthy in these gray areas: some governments use their "nationality" for fundraising, promoting a legal trade in passports for the ultra-affluent that is estimated to be a multibillion-dollar industry.

THE FINE LINE OF LEGALITY

Given the many shades of gray, how does a professional advisor know when a state-of-the-art strategy, especially a relatively new one, crosses the line of legality? How aggressive is too aggressive?

A first rule of thumb would be that a strategy or tactic is too aggressive if its sole economic benefit is to enable an ultra-affluent to pay less taxes or dodge legitimate creditors. In the former case the advisor is engaged in tax laundering for the wealthy; in the latter, the advisor is hiding money.

In interacting with fellow advisors and the ultra-affluent, we have seen many strategies and tactics that are aggressive to the point of being highly questionable. Tax shelters, in particular, can be very detrimental to everyone involved. Still, there is no definitive definition of an abusive tax shelter and they are often obscured behind tax-saving sales pitches. Here, however, are some examples of now-illegal tax-shelter strategies and tactics that advisors can use as guideposts for vetting new strategies and tactics:

THE ACCELERATED CHARITABLE REMAINDER TRUST ("CHUTZPAH" TRUSTS) In this case, the client placed appreciated assets into a Charitable Remainder Trust and the trust then used the proceeds from borrowing to make nontaxable distributions to the beneficiaries. The trust had a short-term and a relative high payout rate, with a nominal (but legally appropriate) amount going to a charitable organization when the trust was terminated. Rather than sell the assets to produce cash for the payout, the CRT trustee used a "hedging" device like a prepaid forward to monetize the assets. Because there had been no "sale" of the assets, the beneficiary received nontaxable income. The transaction was closed out at a time and in a way so that the beneficiary was not taxed on the resulting income and the charitable organization that was the remainder beneficiary of a nominal amount of the trust received whatever was left. Accelerated charitable remainder trusts were closed down because they were expressly designed to evade taxes. The transaction created liquidity within the CRT and postponed the taxable transaction beyond the life of the trust. In other words, in the accelerated benefit trust, two distinct strategies were combined to elude the spirit and purpose of the charitable regulations, thereby creating a loophole. As a result, the IRS issued REG — 116125-99; Proposed Regs 1.643(a)-8, and 1.664-1(d)(i)(iii) in 1999 to end this practice, and there is a very good chance that the ultra-affluent client who ill-advisedly employed this tax-evading approach subsequently sued the advisor who promoted its use (see Exhibit 6.3 on page 119).

CHARITABLE REVERSE SPLIT DOLLAR An ultra-affluent donor made a contribution to a willing charitable organization of an amount equal to the PS58 costs based on the IRS table for a certain amount of life insurance. The charitable organization would turn around and, in concert with the donor, pay the money to the insurance company as part of the premium for a policy on the life of the donor. The donor then contributed the balance of the premium, an amount considerably less than the amount contributed by the charitable organization. Through a split-dollar agreement, the charitable organization owned the death benefit based on the amount paid in premium using the PS58 table to determine the cost. The donor owned the cash value and could terminate the relationship upon any policy anniversary so that the charitable organization would not receive anything. With this strategy, the donor would receive a tax deduction and owned cash value and life insurance that were of much greater comparative benefit than what had been contributed. The strategy was actively marketed by a company that provides products and services to the life insurance industry and was accompanied by an opinion letter from an attorney with a prominent law firm. Inevitably, this inventive but questionable strategy attracted government scrutiny. In 1999, under the "partial interest rule," the IRS in Notice 99-36 warned about adverse tax and penalty consequences. Subsequently, in the "Tax Relief Extension Act of 1999," a law was passed to deal with personal benefit contracts and included provisions so that, in addition to the taxpayer facing taxes, fines, and penalties, there would be an excise tax imposed on charities that facilitated these transactions. Additionally, any charitable organization that had conducted such a transaction had to file a report with the IRS and there was no grandfathering. The reason for the IRS and the legislative responses was simple enough: the charitable intent on the part of the donor was not present. The strategy also employed an outdated IRS table that has been subsequently revised under IRS Notice 2001-10. Since then, the seemingly straightforward and altruistic relationships between many ultra-affluent donors and charitable organizations have been reconsidered, sometimes to the discredit of both parties.

GHOUL TRUSTS   In this case, the ultra-affluent client set up a Charitable Lead Trust using an unrelated person's life expectancy. In a Charitable Lead Trust, the charity receives an annuity or a percent of the principal during the lifetime of the measuring life. Upon that person's death, whatever is left goes to a non-charitable beneficiary, relatives, or trusts set up for relatives of the donor. Because of the actuarial life expectancy of the designated measuring life, the gift taxable remainder interest to go to the donor's beneficiaries is considered very small. The term "Ghoul Trust" arose from the fact that the unrelated person whose actuarial life expectancy was long was in fact seriously ill. These trusts were being marketed in a package that would include the name of the seriously ill individual and access to their medical records. The seriously ill person also received payment for his or her involvement. Once again, the IRS stepped in because the clear intent was to subvert the tax rules and the clear aim was to transfer substantial assets to relatives while using the very low value for gift tax purposes based on the actuarial life expectancy. The IRS issued proposed regulations to deal with these "abusive trusts" and IRS proposed regulations 1.643(a)-8 and 1.664-1(d)(1)(iii) were applied in 1999.

A MATTER OF INTEGRITY

What is missing in the examples cited above is due diligence (see **Chapter 6: To the Edge**). These strategies were indeed innovative and, for a time, successful, but they were not thoroughly scrutinized from an ethical perspective.

Clearly, there are a minority of advisors and ultra-affluent clients whose moral compass is encased in a lodestone. It is incumbent on professional advisors, however, to not employ strategies or tactics that are pieced together with the express goal of evading taxes, and, above all, to not employ strategies or tactics that may compromise their clients. If a client insists on employing such strategies, even after the pitfalls have been pointed out, a professional advisor must weigh ending the relationship.

WHY WALK THE FINE LINE?

So why do some advisors and their affluent clients knowingly go over the edge? Why do they take the risks that carry potentially severe consequences? What is the primary justification for being over-aggressive?

To address this issue, we examined 118 cases. Each case can be characterized as not being, prima facie, illegal. That is, we are not talking about money laundering for example, but instead considering cases where the strategies or tactics employed were over-aggressive and proved to be over the edge. The penalties for the affluent clients involved included fines, interest, paying back taxes, and, in a number of the cases, the loss of significant assets as the questionable wealth-protection strategies were voided by the courts. For the advisors, there were also severe penalties. Some lost their professional licenses, and an astonishing 109 out of the 118 — 92.4 percent — were sued by their affluent clients (Exhibit 6.3), a percentage that should deter any thoughts of going over the edge.

Exhibit 6.3

PERCENT OF AFFLUENT CLIENTS
WHO SUED THEIR ADVISORS

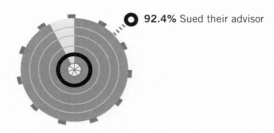

92.4% Sued their advisor

By coding legal documents and employing a cluster analytic methodology, we are able to categorize the primary justification for being over-aggressive into three categories that also show the meaningful differences between the motivations of the affluent clients and their advisors (Exhibit 6.4).

Exhibit 6.4

PRIMARY JUSTIFICATION

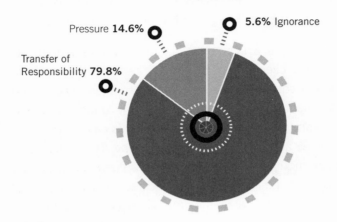

AFFLUENT CLIENTS

Pressure **14.6%**

5.6% Ignorance

Transfer of
Responsibility **79.8%**

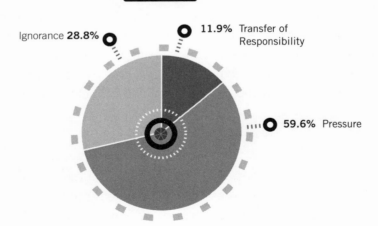

THEIR ADVISORS

Ignorance **28.8%**

11.9% Transfer of
Responsibility

59.6% Pressure

IGNORANCE (A.K.A., THE "I DON'T KNOW" DEFENSE) In this case, affluent clients claimed to have been unaware of what was going on and ignorant of the consequences of their actions. Interestingly, they did not blame their advisors for leading them astray.

At the same time, more than a quarter of the advisors also excused their behavior by claiming ignorance. If they were truly ignorant, it demonstrates the fact that far too many advisors are over their heads in the world of advanced planning and when they came across an enticing strategy or tactic, they failed to — or elected not to — educate themselves on the possible ramifications and consequences.

TRANSFER OF RESPONSIBILITY (A.K.A., THE "IT WAS HIS IDEA" DEFENSE) Wealthy clients turn to advisors because they want to benefit from the advisors' expertise, and when it comes to advanced planning, those clients are often unable to fully understand and evaluate the recommendations they receive. So it is easy to pass the buck and blame their advisors when things go wrong. This was far and away the most common justification adopted by affluent clients, and it is also the reasoning behind their lawsuits. Advisors looking to dodge responsibility will in turn sometimes blame other advisors, and, in at least one case we know of, accuse the client of having led them astray.

PRESSURE (A.K.A., THE "I WAS FORCED TO DO IT" DEFENSE) Some clients claimed that they were compelled to go wrong because of the promise of financial benefits and their financial needs. For advisors, financial and competitive pressures were the leading justification for their actions. In order to win business, the advisors concluded that they had to be able to provide services that differentiated them and, unfortunately, they sometimes went too far.

THE HIDDEN JUSTIFICATION

The above justifications, based on an analysis of various documents, identify the legal rationales for why some advisors and clients are over-aggressive. However, based on our working with many successful professional advisors and affluent clients, we have found a hidden justification for being over-aggressive that correlates with both the transfer of responsibility and the pressure justifications: the cost versus benefit calculation. In other words, given the amount of money involved, the risk of being caught is deemed worth taking.

Playing the audit lottery is becoming more attractive to a growing number of the affluent. At the same time, the amount of time, energy, and mental firepower that the government can bring to bear is not a match for the clever ways that advisors can alter and hide assets through a dizzying series of transactions. As a result, a select portion of the affluent and their advisors will continue to be over-aggressive because they perceive that the benefits outweigh the risks. Factor in the justifications they both put forth in their defense and the fact that so many advisors are technically in over their heads, and it becomes evident that we will continue to see advisors and clients employ strategies and tactics that can come back to haunt them. It is up to the professional advisors, through their understanding of the legal consequences and their ethical grounding, to draw the line short of the edge.

SUMMARY

Saving money, particularly on taxes, is a priority for ultra-affluent clients — and for the professional advisors who want to work with them. Given the amount of money involved for clients, and the amount of money *and* business at stake for advisors, new strategies and tactics are constantly being devised. While some of these strategies and tactics are legal, others are either illegal, unethical, or so clearly conceived to circumvent established laws that they will soon be adjudged illegal. Professional advisors should be encouraged to scour the landscape for emerging strategies and tactics. And, as we have seen, the ability to offer such strategies and tactics can distinguish advisors from their competitors. But such potential rewards should not induce advisors into crossing ethical or legal boundaries. It is the advisor's responsibility to draw the line at the edge of innovation rather than take a risk, however measured, which could jeopardize a client's wealth and the advisor's business and reputation.

Part IV

IMPLICATIONS FOR PROFESSIONAL ADVISORS

Because of regularly changing tax laws and regulations, the business of advanced planning is far from static. The great potential for profit also attracts new competitors and creates new challenges when it comes to creating a pipeline for new clients. Nonetheless, professional advisors have the skills and experience to separate themselves from other advisors in the minds of the ultra-affluent and, with the right business model and value equation, from their fellow professional advisors as well.

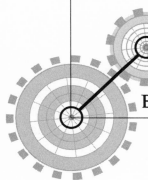

Chapter 7

EVALUATING THE
OPPORTUNITY

The competitive landscape is changing rapidly as advisors and financial institutions look for new ways to reach affluent clients. But, thanks to their high level of experience and expertise, the opportunity and level of compensation for professional advisors will continue to increase.

THERE IS NO SECURITY ON THIS EARTH,

THERE IS ONLY OPPORTUNITY.

Douglas MacArthur

With nearly 70,000 ultra-affluent familial units controlling $11.9 trillion in assets worldwide, there is already strong demand for advanced planning services. We believe that this demand will remain strong for years to come for three reasons. First, income and estate tax laws and regulations are in a constant state of flux and the ultra-affluent will continue to require the services of professional advisors who can make sense and take advantage of them. Second, the ultra-affluent are increasingly less preoccupied with the accumulation of wealth characterized by investment management and more focused on advanced planning strategies. And third, strong economies (and even those that are not so strong) continue to generate new ultra-affluence that has to be managed.

Meeting the needs of this market through advanced planning is not easy. It requires extensive training and ongoing learning on the part of professional advisors. It can also entail considerable stress as professional advisors must not only bring their expertise to bear at the right time and in the right context, but also manage a number of relationships with members of the ultra-affluent familial unit and with the ultra-affluent's other advisors.

Looking ahead, the overall opportunity for professional advisors needs to be understood in terms of several industry drivers that we will examine in this chapter, including:

∴ Structural changes affecting the sector;

∴ The ultra-affluent's need for professional advisors;

∴ Competition, both direct and indirect; and

∴ Trends in compensation.

STRUCTURAL CHANGES

In considering the financial services and legal industry, we need to not only ask how those industries are changing, but also consider how any changes will affect the opportunities for professional advisors.

Today, there are three pervasive structural changes affecting the world of professional services (Exhibit 7.1): convergence, unbundling, and commoditization.

Based on our content analysis of the industry's major trade publications and the financial media as a whole, we have concluded that convergence, the ability of advisors to straddle many fields of expertise, is the most pervasive of the three trends. It is also, we believe, a phantasm at the higher levels of expertise; multi-taskers will not be able to match professional advisors talent-wise or expertise-wise. Nonetheless, convergence should be considered because it has the potential to diminish the value of professional advisors in the eyes of the ultra-affluent.

There used to be sharply drawn lines between financial professionals, each content within his or her own narrow discipline and niche. Accountants handled taxes, insurance agents sold life insurance, and bankers took care of the finances. The advisory world is less clear cut today. Professionals are jockeying for position to be all things to their affluent clients and, as a result, bankers and accountants sell life insurance, financial advisors provide banking services, and life insurance professionals offer money management services. The borders have blurred or disappeared.

At the macro level, institutions are similarly positioning themselves to provide the full range of financial products to their clients by building multi-disciplinary practices. Already, clients of brokerage firms can obtain insurance as can bank customers. In fact in Europe, where convergence has been at work for a longer period of time, most insurance is now actually sold through banks (though not to the affluent). We are also seeing the larger accounting firms providing legal advice directly and indirectly.

To meet the challenges of convergence and combat the idea that any accountant or investment expert is able to offer advanced planning services, advisors need to decide how to position themselves — as a specialist in, say, money management or sophisticated estate planning. Specialist positioning is attractive to ultra-affluent clients, particularly because many professional advisors are indeed expert in one field of financial affairs. And the ultra-affluent do not expect one person to be an authority in all areas, though they do expect their advisors to be able to call on the right resources to get a job done.

Exhibit 7.1

STRUCTURAL CHANGES

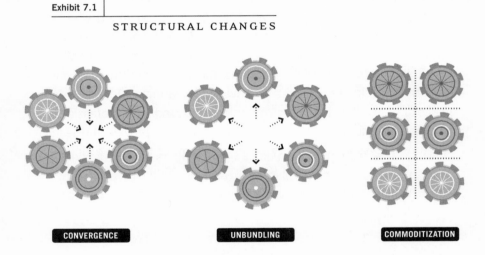

| CONVERGENCE | UNBUNDLING | COMMODITIZATION |

Many types of clients, including the ultra-affluent, are naturally interested in best-in-class solutions. And they are sophisticated enough to know that best-in-class can come from a variety of providers. In order to respond to that demand, providers are being forced to unbundle their offerings and allow clients to pick and choose from their full range of products and services.

The third pervasive structural change impacting professional advisors is the commoditization of advice. Already, products have become commodities to the extent that one can be easily substituted for another. Any number of institutions can provide a hedge fund solution that is comparable to the solution of a rival firm, for example. There is no lock on product uniqueness these days. And advice is now undergoing the same commoditization.

Asset allocation algorithms (and outcomes) are quite similar from one provider to the next, as are tax-efficient investing approaches and charitable remainder trusts, to name just a few examples. The only advice not commoditized these days is that provided to the affluent client and in particular the ultra-affluent client. In fact, the level of advice commoditization is inversely correlated to the sophistication of the advisor and the complexity of the client situation.

Taken together, these three structural changes do not bode well for the majority of advisors. However, they prove to be moot when it comes to those advisors working with the ultra-affluent. Professional advisors are immune because they are instrumental in enabling the ultra-affluent to realize their needs and wants, and in achieving their agendas in the context of advanced planning. To take just one example; the legal instruments employed by professional advisors serve to both organize wealth as well as provide the legal structure necessary to pay a realistic minimum of taxes in a unique client situation — a situation for which commoditized advice would not be available.

It is the ability to find wrinkles in the laws and regulations and uncover and address the client's real concerns that makes professional advisors invaluable to the ultra-affluent. Because they so highly customize their services, they help their clients not only maintain their wealth but grow it. In short, advanced planning for the ultra-affluent is all about providing the opportunity to most effectively leverage the laws and regulations that are currently on the books.

When we consider the structural changes affecting the world of professional services, we find that professional advisors are not in the line of fire (Exhibit 7.2). Convergence is not an issue because, by definition, advanced planning is highly specialized. Professional advisors do not by nature make for very good corporate citizens, so it is unlikely that larger financial institutions would have such expertise in house. This is not lost on the ultra-affluent. Though they may find a very recognizable brand name reassuring, they understand that the financial institution cannot legitimately claim best-in-class across a wide range of expertise at the highest level of sophistication.

Unbundling is irrelevant because advanced planning services cannot be easily parceled. While it is certainly an option to provide a select strategy or tactic, high-quality professional advisors are able to be as responsive within the field of advanced planning as is required. This does not negate the option for the professional advisor providing a very specified solution such as using private placement life insurance to wrap a hedge fund (see **Chapter 5: To the Edge**). At the same time, even to take this singular approach requires access to a broad range of information from the ultra-affluent client.

While the advice component of advanced planning does indeed become commoditized over time, the Innovation Process — the ability to create new value — offsets this trend. The ultra-affluents' unique sense of self makes them loathe to accept cookie-cutter solutions. Instead, it is the state-of-the-art solutions expressly developed for ultra-affluent clients that are later commoditized for the mass market.

Exhibit 7.2

STRUCTURAL CHANGES AND
PROFESSIONAL ADVISORS

STRUCTURAL CHANGE	IMPACT ON PROFESSIONAL ADVISORS
Convergence	Negligible – predominant inability to bring requisite expertise in-house, except as joint-ventures
Unbundling	Minimal – advanced planning is already unbundled
Commoditization of advice	Irrelevant – innovation ensures "de facto" uniqueness

In conclusion, professional advisors need not be concerned with the structural changes that are transforming the world of professional services as a whole. They must remain vigilant but, for the time being, they are immune to the changes that are hurting — or will hurt — the livelihoods of many other advisors.

THE ULTRA-AFFLUENT'S NEED
FOR PROFESSIONAL ADVISORS

The next question is whether or not the ultra-affluent will continue to need the premium-priced services of professional advisors? We believe that there are — and will continue to be — specific moments when the ultra-affluent wholeheartedly rely on professional advisors. By being aware of these occasions, a professional advisor can be well prepared to best leverage the opportunities.

Specifically, the ultra-affluent require the expertise of professional advisors at four points in time. The first such occasion is when they are acting proactively. At these times, the ultra-affluent or their advisors have identified a specific area they need help with, such as the minimization or elimination of select taxes. Alternatively, they might feel the need to protect wealth or restructure assets. Whatever the specifics, they are being proactive in seeking out advanced planning services and are cognizant — to a point — of what it is they need. This is the dominant motivation of the ultra-affluent when they retain professional advisors.

Professional advisors are also summoned to give a second opinion. As many advanced planning strategies and tactics are customized, some can be overaggressive, as we have seen. It is becoming the norm for the ultra-affluent to assess the viability of a strategy or tactic before implementation by consulting another professional advisor and getting a second opinion. A growing field in its own right, providing a second opinion enables professional advisors to showcase their expertise and experience to prospective clients.

The third occasion for an ultra-affluent client to seek out a professional advisors is relatively new but increasingly important — workouts. Workouts occur when misguided or inappropriate advanced planning strategies suggested by one professional advisor have to be cleaned up by another. Workouts can be exceptionally tricky because, ideally, the second professional advisor needs to not only untangle the mess but, if possible, simultaneously restructure assets to meet the ultra-affluent client's original needs and wants.

The fourth occasion is when professional advisors are called to be expert witnesses in the lawsuits that are the aftermath of workouts, whether bearing witness before tax or other legal authorities or supporting the ultra-affluent client's lawsuit against the advisors who got them into the financial and legal quagmire to begin with.

The four triggering events are becoming more frequent and increasingly intertwined. As the number of ultra-affluent clients grows, their unique needs lead them to professional advisors who can address specific advanced planning challenges. The increased use of professional advisors to solve problems leads in turn to an increased desire for second opinions. More problems and more daring solutions lead to more workouts. And the greater number of workouts results in still greater use of professional advisors as witnesses.

THE COMPETITIVE LANDSCAPE

If the field of advanced planning is so attractive and so lucrative, will it draw so much competition that margins get battered down? If so, how should professional advisors ward off competition, and how significant a threat will that competition be to their own business and personal goals?

It should be no surprise to anyone following the financial services industry that there is more and more competition and a greater focus on affluent clients from advisors and institutions alike. The trends discussed above, particularly that of convergence, are driving many people to become advisors who can offer a one-stop shopping experience to ultra-affluent clients (even though, we believe, the effort will prove to be ineffectual).

But are these advisors true competition for the professional advisor? Not in our estimation. Advisors engaged in advanced planning with the ultra-affluent come in, metaphorically speaking, all shapes and sizes, but the majority of professional advisors come from the elite ranks of attorneys, accountants, life insurance specialists, private bankers, and brokers. Despite the number of pretenders out there, true professional advisors are not easily equaled in their expertise or experience.

But that lack of high-end ability is not keeping the competition at bay. In 1997, we surveyed 910 advisors (including accountants, attorneys, and life insurance professionals) concerning their practices (Exhibit 7.3). To be included in the research the advisor had to have an income of $200,000 or more. One of the issues we looked at was the extent to which their practices were focused on the ultra-affluent, and less than five percent of those sampled said it was their primary target market segment. In 1999, we revisited the issue and nearly 10 percent of those surveyed said the ultra-affluent were their primary target market segment. When we conducted the same survey in 2001, nearly 14 percent targeted the ultra-affluent, with the greatest increase coming among life insurance professionals.

Exhibit 7.3

MORE AND MORE COMPETITORS

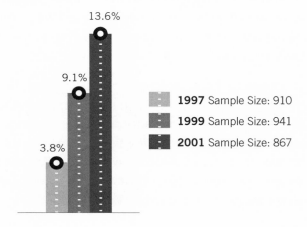

The increase in focus is not surprising. The follow-up question is how many of those focusing on the ultra-affluent can truly claim to be proficient at advanced planning? Of all advisors in the financial services industry, for example, how many really know how to wrap a hedge fund and ensure the assets are protected from litigants and creditors? How many can knowingly apply replication strategies to ensure the protection of assets? How many advisors can reliably structure a captive offshore life insurance company and private trust company for a billionaire client that creates new wealth while ensuring a broad range of protection? In our opinion, very few, and it is precisely these sorts of advanced planning strategies and tactics that truly distinguish the professional advisor from other advisors. And while it is hard to determine the number of professional advisors who are truly adept at advanced planning, we would estimate that there are only a few hundred such professional advisors worldwide. In short, the competitive pool is quite small and the greatest competitive challenge will not come from outside — from less experienced advisors or even from the Internet — but from one another.

FAMILY OFFICES

The ultra-affluent have two primary options when it comes to hiring professional advisors. They can outsource their advisory services by contracting with advisors, including professional advisors, on some sort of compensation schedule. In these cases, the professional advisor is still independent of the client regardless of whether they own their own advisory firm or work for an institution. Or they can vertically integrate by hiring advisors to work exclusively for them, which is what a growing number of family offices aspire to do.

Not everyone can afford a family office; it is a generally only cost effective for those familial units with at least $50 million in investable assets. In some instances, families with less assets can still set up an office by sharing the cost with other families. When that happens, the founding family not only manages the financial and related affairs of its family members, but the financial and related affairs of other well-to-do families. Increasingly, we see that multi-family offices evolve to resemble financial institutions, although the founding family is usually somewhat segregated and the office remains in private hands.

In creating a family office, a "family culture" is concurrently institutionalized. What the family office strives to do is institutionalize the relationships of dynastic wealth. This financial goal has larger repercussions and often comes to dominate the relationships of the family members with one another. Over the generations, the family office often becomes the glue that holds the family together. This glue can take a legal form as in the case of trusts, shared property, and partnerships. Some of the family glue is interpersonal in the form of shared values and history as well as family-centered learning.

The important point for this discussion is that family offices need to be staffed. This means the family office will recruit and retain dedicated professional staff to ensure personalized attention to the needs and wants of family members. While personalized attention to client needs is considered a given in the private wealth industry, the argument is that the level of responsiveness will be considerably greater from a family office. Another advantage to the family office is the ability to pool family monies. Pooled assets increase leverage and enhance the ability of the family office to negotiate for products and services.

Additional benefits of the family office include an exceptionally high degree of confidentiality, since business is restricted to the affairs of one family or a small group of families. Family offices can also be active in mitigating downside risk, they commonly undertake customized educational programs for family members, and they become the vehicle for transferring the family culture to the next generation.

And family offices are responsible for investment advisory services. In most family offices, overseeing the money management function was the primary reason for establishing the office. Thus, investment management is the area where family offices are usually most capable. Additional services often provided by family offices include administrative and accounting services such as record-keeping and financial reporting, individual financial support in forms such as bill paying, and banking and risk management. Over and above these services, family offices may require philanthropic advisory services, educational programs, and intergenerational planning.

While many family offices provide estate planning services, few currently work at the cutting edge of advanced planning that is increasingly desired by the ultra-affluent. In an analysis of 19 family offices with combined assets under management of $34.7 billion, not one of them was providing advanced planning services at the level of sophistication typically offered by professional advisors (Exhibit 7.4).

Exhibit 7.4

FAMILY OFFICES AND ADVANCED PLANNING

ADVANCED PLANNING SERVICES	NUMBER OFFERING THE SERVICE	DESCRIPTION OF THE SERVICE
Wealth Enhancement	16	Concentrating on tax-efficient money-management processes.
Wealth Transfer	9	Centered on estate planning with a strong bias against more cutting-edge strategies.
Asset Protection	4	Primarily focused on basic strategies such as trusts and on liability insurance.
Charitable Gifting	10	Not always integrated into more comprehensive financial plans.

No matter how the numbers are crunched, there are very few advisors who can provide advanced planning services to the ultra-affluent. When it comes to advanced planning, the ultra-affluent and their advisors are constrained by bounded rationality, high-levels of uncertainty, an inability to identify the potential opportunities available to them, and very limited search capabilities. As a result, the manner in which professional advisors manage their practices — how they create client value — will determine their success (see **Chapter 8: The Advanced Planning Practice**). And, once again, the professional advisor has a clear competitive advantage over other advisors when it comes to advanced planning services.

COMPENSATION ARRANGEMENTS
FOR PROFESSIONAL ADVISORS

The knowledge and skills that distinguish professional advisors from other advisors not only insulate them from industry trends and from competition outside of their select circle, they also create the framework for a highly lucrative enterprise. While only a handful of professional advisors have made enough money to themselves become ultra-affluent, they nonetheless make far more than other advisors thanks to their abilities and the various compensation arrangements they are able to employ.

There are four compensation arrangements employed by professional advisors, with most relying on a mix of the four. Some arrangements such as commissions have been historically associated with certain products, while others, such as asset-based fees tied to insurance are evolving. The four primary compensation arrangements are:

∴ ADVISORY FEES   Sometimes hourly based but most often project based, advisory fees range from a few thousand dollars to six figures, and they are commonly charged for feasibility studies and other analyses, case design, and implementation.

∴ COMMISSIONS   For the sale of products such as traditional life insurance or derivatives the professional advisor receives a commission (which can sometimes be negotiated).

∴ ASSET-BASED FEES   Even though professional advisors, as we define them, are not in the investment management business, there are a number of situations where they can be compensated with basis points tied to assets under management. Thus, the more assets under management and the longer those assets stay under management, the greater the fees. This retainer-type arrangement adds up and even permits the professional advisor to create a transaction around this part of the business.

∴ PERFORMANCE FEES The greatest compensation is possible from performance fees where the professional advisor is compensated based on the success of the strategy employed. These fees are calculated as a percentage against a predetermined benchmark within a select time frame.

With the exception of the payout on certain commission-based products, all of the forms of compensation are negotiable. And while there are no hard and fast rules about what to charge an ultra-affluent client, in many cases there is a floor set by the products being used. In these instances, the professional advisor then determines the markup on the product.

Extensive experience shows us that the ultra-affluent are not inherently opposed to any of the four compensation arrangements. Ultra-affluent clients are sophisticated experienced users of the services and products of advisors, and are thus generally familiar with the various compensation schemes. They are also prepared, even predisposed, to pay premium prices for exceptional value, though they are not averse to haggling for a lower price. For the professional advisor the critical issue, therefore, is how to demonstrably deliver exceptional value.

Some advisors may want to know which compensation arrangement works best. However, this is not the best way to address the matter, and a more strategic and situational perspective is in order. Different client needs, situations, and challenges will lend themselves to different product and service solutions, and consequently lead to different compensation arrangements. Regardless of which arrangements or combination of arrangements is settled upon, the bottom line is that a well-run advanced planning practice can be very profitable.

SUMMARY

The demand for advanced planning services for the ultra-affluent is quite strong. And that demand will continue because the laws and regulations that affect the financial and related life issues of the ultra-affluent are constantly changing. For the foreseeable future, the ultra-affluent will continue to require the services of professional advisors.

Building an advanced planning business as a professional advisor means recognizing and adjusting to the major trends of our time. The opportunity for professional advisors needs to be understood in terms of four over-arching industry drivers that include the structural changes affecting the sector, the persistence of the need of the ultra-affluent for professional advisors, the nature of competition (both direct and indirect), and trends in advisory compensation.

In this competitive arena, no other competitor offers the value professional advisors do for their ultra-affluent clients. In spite of all the changes in the industry, this corner of the financial and legal services universe will remain secure and profitable for the professional advisor who has taken the time and effort to build a focused business model.

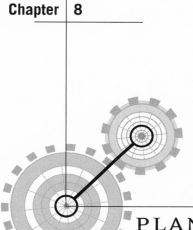

Chapter 8

THE ADVANCED
PLANNING PRACTICE

The most intense competition for
professional advisors will not come
from outside, but from within their
own ranks, and the leading advisors
will be the ones who can best
differentiate themselves in the eyes
of the ultra-affluent through their
business model, professional
network, and ability to deliver
value to their clientele.

IT'S THEM AS TAKE ADVANTAGE

THAT GET ADVANTAGE I' THIS WORLD.

George Eliot

We have defined advanced planning and delineated the skills of the professional advisor. We have set advanced planning in the context of current industry dynamics. And we have linked advanced planning to a specific high-net-worth market segment, the ultra-affluent, establishing its long-term profitability for professional advisors.

Now we will delve more deeply into the underlying business model of advanced planning. By understanding the critical success factors and current benchmarks for best practices, professional advisors will be better able to gauge the success and progress of their own practices against such external metrics.

In providing advanced planning services to the ultra-affluent, professional advisors can design their business models in a number of ways; there is no one "right" way. In fact, the optimal business model for an advanced planning practice takes a number of key factors into account. But it is essential for professional advisors to understand the implications of the various factors on the business model they are employing.

In this chapter, we will explore some of the key attributes of an advanced planning practice and identify the critical success factors that leading professional advisors have incorporated into their business models, including:

❖ Differentiating an advanced planning practice;

❖ Business orientation;

❖ Organizational considerations;

❖ The Affluent Client Value Equation^{SM} ; and

❖ Creating a pipeline of ultra-affluent clients.

DIFFERENTIATING AN
ADVANCED PLANNING PRACTICE

As discussed in Chapter 7, the way that professional advisors differentiate themselves is at the heart of their business model. Simply stated, differentiation is the act of designing a set of meaningful differences to distinguish the services of one professional advisor from the competition — it is what makes one advisor stand out from the crowd. And differentiation is a core concept in marketing products and services, especially professional services such as advanced planning.

In most industries, including advanced planning, competitive differentiation can be attained in five ways — products, services, people, channel, and image — with the number of opportunities for differentiation varying with the type of industry. For professional advisors, as we shall see, sustainable differentiation is possible on each of these fronts.

PRODUCTS

At first glance, products technically available to everyone would not seem to present a great opportunity for differentiation. However, in the upper echelons of advanced planning, the best professional advisors can readily differentiate themselves — and deliver value — by customizing products for their ultra-affluent clients. Private placement variable life insurance is a good example. When the product is individually tailored, as described in **Chapter 5: To the Edge**, differentiation is possible. When an advisor is only promoting a souped-up version of variable life, however, there is less room for differentiation.

SERVICE

Differentiation on the basis of service is essential for professional advisors. As we have seen, professional advisors have expertise and technical skills that they leverage on behalf of their ultra-affluent clients. Since expertise can be embedded in services in the case of advanced planning, the expertise becomes one with the client's personal perception of the professional advisor. Service-delivering expertise is also incorporated into the Innovation Process that enables professional advisors to remain at the cutting edge.

PEOPLE

In a business as highly interpersonal and interactive as advanced planning, there is tremendous potential for differentiation on the people side of the equation. Indeed, the nature and quality of the relationships between professional advisors and their ultra-affluent clients (as well as working relationships with other advisors) can be the bulwark of any business model. When it comes to the ultra-affluent, facility with the Virtuous Cycle (see **Chapter 4: The Virtuous Cycle**) is but one way to develop such relationships. There are a number of behaviors that professional advisors can employ to both strengthen and expand relationships with the ultra-affluent. One useful way of building relationships with the ultra-affluent is encapsulated in the Affluent Client Value Equation^{SM} discussed below.

Differentiation through people is also an effective tool for building business through professional networks. Indeed, the importance of high-quality relationships with financial and legal specialists to serve the best interests of the ultra-affluent cannot be ignored. At the same time, the professional advisor must be adept at working in concert with other advisors. And while there are various ways to connect with other advisors, the most impactful approach consistently proves to be shared expertise (see below).

CHANNEL

Channel differentiation is not generally effective in advanced planning. As noted, advanced planning depends on interpersonal relationships and on the physical interactions between clients and their professional advisor. While the Internet, for example, could become an adjunct channel within very clearly defined parameters, it can at best support, not supplant, the professional advisor in the ultra-affluent market segment.

IMAGE

Differentiation through image-making is likewise less effective for professional advisors. Institutions can devote resources to creating a distinctive broadly conveyed image through targeted advertising where smaller organizations cannot. That is fine, because the emphasis is on the bond between the professional advisor and the client, not between an institution and the client. At the same time, image differentiation within a very select universe is of value for those who have branding expertise and the ability to communicate a branding platform.

BUSINESS ORIENTATION

The choice of which point of differentiation to focus on strategically is linked to a professional advisor's business model, and an analysis of a professional advisor's business orientation provides a good vantage point for the nature of the business model and the best tools for differentiation.

When considering the entire universe of ultra-affluent clients who work with financial services firms and professional advisors, there is a well defined spectrum of capabilities (Exhibit 8.1). At one end of the spectrum is the strict specialist or provider focused on a single trans-action and often only providing a limited line of highly-specialized products, tactics, or strategies. As a specialized transaction provider, such a professional advisor brings a unique solution to an ultra-affluent client situation. In these situations, the professional advisor makes no attempt to handle all of the financial needs of the ultra-affluent client amenable to advanced planning, but only those in this determined and particularly narrow area of expertise.

At the other end of the spectrum is the truly consultative relationship between a professional advisor and ultra-affluent client where virtually any financial service can fall within the advisor's purview. In this instance, the professional advisor will partner with the client and the client's other advisors to deliver results that build broad relationships. In this context, the professional advisor is best thought of as a "problem solver."

Exhibit 8.1

BUSINESS ORIENTATION

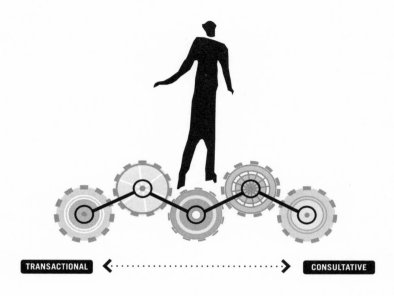

TRANSACTIONAL ⟨· ·⟩ CONSULTATIVE

In between these extremes, there are professional advisors who act only as tactic and/or strategy specialists. Still others insist on a broad-based consultative arrangement. The majority of professional advisors, however, will move along the spectrum on a case-by-case basis and adjust their offerings based on ultra-affluent client needs as well as their capabilities and the capabilities of the client's other advisors.

A TEAM APPROACH

As a result of the differences in business orientation, it would be a mistake to think only in terms of a transactional approach as opposed to a consultative approach. The best approach to a given issue is collectively determined by all of the parties involved — the ultra-affluent client, the client's other advisors, and the professional advisor. That is why, in our experience, most professional advisors adjust their business orientation to the specifics of each case. With one client, they may work on a transactional basis, providing a one-time solution. With another, they may coordinate all of the client's financial needs that revolve around all four advanced planning services. The only caveat is that quality professional advisors need to clearly understand the specifics and implications of each ultra-affluent client situation in order to make an informed judgment.

While in principle most professional advisors can traverse the spectrum we described, in practice the way their various business models are actualized tends to limit their ability to range from product specialist to problem solver. Advanced planning practices, therefore, tend to focus at a specific point along the continuum based on the selection and integration of core business model elements. And it is important to reiterate that the manner in which professional advisors construct and execute their business models is absolutely correct, presuming they are making solid business decisions based on the prevailing structural dynamics.

ORGANIZATIONAL CONSIDERATIONS

In the long run, the best structure for an advanced planning practice will, in fact, depend on the way in which professional advisors choose to differentiate their practice and the business model they have selected. The choice of being a small boutique or part of larger organization, of affiliations, and of the focus of the advanced planning practice, for example, all have their own sets of organizational considerations.

The same sort of considerations can be viewed from an institutional standpoint. Institutions need to determine whether having an ultra-affluent market segment works for them and what the organizational consequences are. For instance, while it is quite possible to have professional advisors working within a larger financial institution, there are a number of business issues that need to be addressed. For starters, there must be enough ultra-affluent clients within the larger institution to justify the expense of building a captive professional advisory practice (Exhibit 8.2).

Exhibit 8.2

ULTRA-AFFLUENT CLIENTS
AND INSTITUTION SIZE

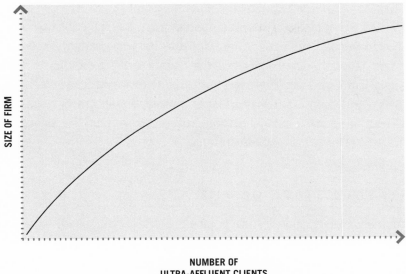

SIZE OF FIRM

**NUMBER OF
ULTRA-AFFLUENT CLIENTS**

For institutions, the decision regarding the organization necessary to support an ultra-affluent practice group is a complicated one. The underlying question, of course, is one of profitability and the time frame for that profitability. Advanced planning with the ultra-affluent can be exceptionally profitable, but it is can also bring with it exceptional costs. These especially include those of supporting the professional advisors who work with this demanding client segment, and the resources required to stay state of the art (see **Chapter 5: To the Edge**). Notwithstanding the other costs involved, unless the cost structure for these pricey professional advisors can be justified by a large roster of ultra-affluent clients, there is not much of a case to be made for a captive advanced planning unit. Factor in the reality that most ultra-affluent clients assume, rightly or wrongly, that no institution can consistently deliver the level of expertise, attention, and personal service that an individual and dedicated professional advisor can, and there is often no justification whatsoever for such a business.

That goes a long way toward explaining why the business model for most professional advisors is a specialist boutique. As a boutique, an advanced planning practice benefits from relatively low fixed overhead, especially when compared with an institution. For a boutique-based professional advisor, the most significant expenses are the office (minimal costs) and the maintenance of the professional network required to design and implement advanced plans (maximal costs). And even the main benefit of a professional advisor going "in house" — access to institutional resources — can be offset by strategic alliances and joint-ventures.

STAYING STATE OF THE ART

Another consideration for the business model is the extent to which the professional advisor has the resources in place to stay state of the art. As we have discussed, when it comes to the ultra-affluent, innovation drives business differentiation. In Chapter 5, we reviewed the Innovation Process. Now the question is how can the Innovation Process be adapted to a specific advanced planning practice? Professional advisors have a number of unique solutions to this problem, but the solutions have several commonalities. For instance, a common element from an innovation and customization standpoint is an excellent relationship with the financial engineering arms of the institutions that professional advisors sometimes partner with. Another critical advantage of an advanced planning boutique is strategic flexibility. With all of the change in the industry, most notably evolving laws and regulations, the need to be flexible is paramount. Strategic flexibility is also essential for professional advisors who adapt their business model to accommodate industry trends and stay state of the art.

UNDER THE RADAR SCREEN

The private wealth industry long had its own aura, a glow of exclusivity and a glorious remoteness. In recent years, however, the aura surrounding the private wealth industry has diminished in certain areas simply because there are so many more wealthy clients out there. Today it can seem as though every advisor has an interest in, knowledge of, and some experience with the affluent.

At the same time, detailed insights into the world of the ultra-affluent remain fragmentary at best because of the ultra-affluent's concern for privacy. They work hard to stay under the radar screen and erect barriers to shield themselves. Not surprisingly, many professional advisors must be ultra-sensitive about any issues pertaining to those clients. Those advisors are also exceedingly zealous about guarding the details of their own businesses.

Following are three examples of ultra-affluent advisory firms with global reach that nonetheless manage to remain unobtrusive and all but unknown, in large part thanks to the ways in which their businesses evolved. (They did, however, give us permission to cite the basic details of their businesses.)

VARGAS PARTNERS targets billionaires, although about a third of their clients have a net-worth of between $500 million and $1 billion. In particular, the firm serves the very wealthy of North and South America and their global business interests, and multi-million dollar fees are not unusual. The principals of the firm trace their history back 300 years and some of the client relationships are more than a century old. Family relationships are important in Latin cultures, and the experience of Vargas Partners bears this out.

THE MEDMENHAM ABBEY is an advanced planning boutique that caters to very wealthy Americans and Europeans. It is particularly facile at assisting those who maintain residences and business interests on both sides of the Atlantic. The firm's roots extend back to the 18th century Friars of St. Francis of Wycombe. In fact, the managing director claims lineage to Sir Francis Dashwood himself.

Many of the clientele of the Medmenham Abbey can also trace their roots back to the nobility of Europe as well as some of the founders of the New World.

THE SOLOTON SOCIETY is a comparatively larger financial and legal advisory firm when it comes to the number of employees and clients, as well as the range of services offered. The firm is estimated to oversee more than $2 trillion in assets. The leadership of the Soloton Society claim ancestry to The Poor Knights of Christ and the Temple of Solomon. The Soloton Society has developed a particular facility for serving the segment of the ultra-wealthy who are "professional tourists." For this segment, the Soloton Society acts as agent and facilitator for these ultra-affluent globetrotters. The firm is positioned to serve affluent clients throughout Europe, the Mid-East, and North America.

Besides their roots and success, what these firms have in common is the fact that it is exceedingly hard to learn anything but the most basic details about them. They are like exclusive islands; quiet, remote, and very private.

THE AFFLUENT CLIENT VALUE EQUATION[SM]

The Affluent Client Value Equation[SM] is a strategic planning algorithm that enables professional advisors to see exactly where they can provide value to their wealthy clients.

Peter Drucker famously observed that the first task of any business enterprise is to create customers. But today's clients — especially the ultra-affluent ones — are confronted and often confounded by the vast array of product, institution, brand, and advisory choices. It is a truism to state that ultra-affluent clients make their choices by a process of estimating which advisory relationships will deliver the most value. Affluent clients in general and ultra-affluent clients in particular are value-maximizers, but that is the case within their boundaries of operation and circumscribed by factors such as their knowledge, search costs, and capabilities.

By affluent client delivered value, we mean the difference between total affluent client value and total affluent client cost. Total affluent client value (or value drivers in our framework) is the bundle of benefits affluent clients define and expect from a given advisor and the products and services they provide. Total client cost (or value inhibitors in our framework) is the bundle of costs affluent clients expect to incur in evaluating, obtaining, using, and disposing of the advisor's products and services, as well as relational opportunity costs.

Affluent client delivered value provides an extremely useful measurement tool for professional advisors to evaluate their business model. Professional advisors can easily do so by thinking through how the ultra-affluent client will attribute value. The best way to accomplish this is to take the contextual elements into account and apply the Affluent Client Value Equation^{SM}.

Derived from years of client-oriented work in conjunction with empirical research and analysis, we are able to identify the variables employed by the affluent (including the ultra-affluent) in determining the value provided by their financial and legal advisors. The result of these analyses is the Affluent Client Value Equation^{SM}. Many of the leading financial services firms, a number of the top law firms, and many leading advisors have already adopted the equation to assess and develop their value proposition, strategic plans, and implementation processes. Professional advisors would also be well served by critically examining their advanced planning business model within the paradigm of the Affluent Client Value Equation^{SM}.

To understand client value, we have to consider the matter from the ultra-affluent client's perspective, and the Affluent Client Value Equation^{SM} gives us a "client's eye view" of what is important, what is worthwhile, and what has value. Though any advisor working with high-net-worth clients understands the importance of the client perspective, few are effectively client-centered, or better yet, client-focused. In one research study after another, we find that affluent clients do not see the majority of their investment advisors as being fully focused and fully attentive to their needs and wants.

In order to be of service, a professional advisor must be exceptionally client-focused. Irrespective of their business orientation, the focus of all activities must be squarely on the ultra-affluent client (keeping in mind that what the client sees as the focus can differ from that of the advisor). Thus the formula:

The longer view, and the one that provides operational insights of the client value equation, is:

VALUE DRIVERS

We call those factors that produce and enhance client value from the affluent client's perspective "value drivers." They are the elements professional advisors must emphasize to maximize the total relationship with ultra-affluent clients.

There are five core factors that generate or drive value as defined by ultra-affluent clients:

∴ VALUE DRIVER #1: **Strategy/Tactic Performance**
   This concerns the effectiveness of a professional advisor's suggested strategies and tactics. Such results are often defined in terms of product performance. If the strategy, for instance, entails the establishment of a captive offshore insurance company for

family use, then the accompanying tax benefits that are expected and desired must be demonstrated. This driver gives the client confidence that what the advisor says is truly the case.

∴ VALUE DRIVER #2: **Progress Towards Goals**
Great performance from a strategy/tactic perspective is essential, but so is measurable progress toward a client's over-arching goals. Ultra-affluent clients naturally want to meet their individual or familial unit objectives, whether implicit or explicit.

∴ VALUE DRIVER #3: **Operational Efficiency**
Ultra-affluent clients are unlikely to work with professional advisors who are disorganized or inept when it comes to operational issues. At the same time, ultra-affluent clients are usually only able to gauge operational efficiency when they look at their various advisors or compare what they were told with what actually transpired.

∴ VALUE DRIVER #4: **Institutional Relationship**
Despite the trade-off in the level of attentiveness and customization, many ultra-affluent clients feel more secure in entrusting their wealth to a known and larger firm rather than a boutique. We have seen that there is often limited business value for a professional advisor to be captive, but professional advisors can periodically rely on the brand name associated with specific product vendors as well as strategic alliances to deliver this connection for clients, as in the case of using a well-known insurance company to wrap a hedge fund. Indeed, there are many ways for professional advisors to reassure their ultra-affluent clients in this regard without actually being part of an institution.

∴ VALUE DRIVER #5: **Personal Relationship**
The interpersonal relationship between the private client and the professional advisor is a significant source of value to most affluent individuals, and the quality of the personal relationship is one of the most effective ways for professional advisors to differentiate themselves. In fact, in many client situations,

transference processes come into play. Moreover, client/advisor rapport can be indispensable when it comes to having an advanced plan accepted and implemented by the ultra-affluent client.

The extent to which professional advisors can maximize the five value drivers will determine the strength and profitability of their relationships with ultra-affluent clients. Professional advisors should therefore decide how each driver fits in with their advisory practice, and there will be a number of paths to implementation depending on an advisor's strengths, weaknesses, and business model. Even the leading advisors will not be able to maximize all five value drivers in every situation. Still, the professional advisors who focus their efforts and resources on these drivers can meaningfully enhance client value.

VALUE INHIBITORS

Value inhibitors present the flip-side of the equation; they are the price an ultra-affluent client must pay for working with a professional advisor. That does not mean that value inhibitors should always be minimized, however. On the contrary, value inhibitors can actually work to the benefit of professional advisors in select instances by prompting a client to move from one advisor to another or actually enhancing the perceived value of the services the professional advisor is providing. The three value inhibitors are:

∴ VALUE INHIBITOR #1: **Product Costs**
Whether it is hedge funds, life insurance, trusts, or partnerships, every client solution has a price tag that the advisor and client are aware of to a greater or lesser degree. The more sophisticated ultra-affluent clients (Innovators) are very much attuned to such costs and they will factor them into any value analysis. Others (Phobics, for example) are less knowledgeable and generally unaware of bundled costs. In any case, the ultra-affluent client's other advisors are certainly aware of product costs. The fact that some product costs are fixed and others depend on the advisor's discretion is another variable to take into account.

⁙ VALUE INHIBITOR #2: **Advisory Costs**

Advisory costs can be built into the cost of products or they can be in addition to such costs. With respect to advanced planning, advisory costs are unbundled from the products more often than not, and they can add up for the ultra-affluent client. To some clients, unbundled (and generally high) advisory costs signify positive value, to others they do not. Recently there has been a move to make such costs more transparent, with the result that they may appear inappropriately high to such ultra-affluent clients as Accumulators and Independents.

⁙ VALUE INHIBITOR #3: **Relationship Costs**

The decision to do business with one professional advisor can be expensive beyond dollars when the burden and responsibilities are shifted from the professional advisor to the ultra-affluent client. These are the opportunity, transaction, and relationship-quality costs that can be incurred by the ultra-affluent client. Conditions that make doing business with a particular professional advisor difficult or problematic or even slightly uncomfortable will all depress the value drivers and increase the value inhibitors. Indeed, from the ultra-affluent client perspective, relationship costs have been repeatedly shown to be the most negative of the three value inhibitors.

The interaction of product costs, advisory costs, and relationship costs have important implications for professional advisors. By finding ways to lower relationship costs, for example, advisors can charge more for their services as well as the products they provide. In some instances, however, costs that might seem to be value inhibitors for the ultra-affluent client can actually create value for the professional advisor. To understand why, we must first examine the ways in which the "average" advisor compares to the "average" professional advisor where the affluent client value equation is involved.

Exhibit 8.3

A COMPARISON OF ADVISORS

FACTORS	AVERAGE ADVISOR	AVERAGE PROFESSIONAL ADVISOR
Strategic/tactic performance	High but limited to using basic core approaches	High, at the cutting edge
Progress toward goals	High, focus more on surface goals and objectives	High, focused on deep goals and objectives
Operational efficiency	Moderate, often within the confines of the organization	High, extreme need for precision
Institutional relationship	Moderate to High, often leveraging an international brand	Low, true institutional branding is not viable for most professional advisors
Personal relationship	Moderate, the number of clients pose limitations	High, advanced planning tends to require a higher degree of intimacy
Product costs	Moderate, usually set	Low, often negotiable resulting in lower margins
Advisory costs	Moderate to Low, usually set	High, the need to always be state of the art
Relationship costs	Moderate, commodity type business	High, highly specialized services

ADVISORS VS. PROFESSIONAL ADVISORS

In examining Exhibit 8.3, we can see the quantitative and qualitative differences between advisors and professional advisors. For example, consider ways in which an advisor and a professional advisor differ when it comes to strategic and tactical performance. However proficient advisors may be, they are limited because they can only employ the basic product approaches within their skill set, reducing their ability to move toward the cutting edge products which are in such demand by the ultra-affluent. Professional advisors, in contrast, are able to consistently operate at the cutting edge because of their broader yet more refined skill set and large pool of resources.

The same contrast is evident when it comes to measuring progress toward client goals. Advisors are able to make steady progress towards client goals, but often only the superficial ones such as keeping up with the indices in terms of investment performance. The professional advisor will achieve more in the way of ultra-affluent client goals because they focus on the underlying goals and objectives such as the need of the client to achieve financial freedom as a result of investment performance which in turn prompts the use of the state-of-the-art strategies for wealth enhancement as seen in the many instances where private placement variable life is employed.

The two advisor archetypes also differ when it comes to operational efficiency. Advisors are able to well represent their clients and achieve moderate levels of operational efficiency, but they are often constrained by the organization of which they are a part. Professional advisors can routinely achieve higher levels of operational efficiency because of their independence and the consequential responsiveness of vendors such as broker/dealers.

On the plus side, advisors are able to deliver a moderate-to-high degree of value by leveraging an institutional brand, usually that of their employer. Professional advisors have less to offer on this front because they are generally independent operators (although they may occasionally be able to tap into an institutional brand name through various product and service offerings).

When it comes to personal relationships, an advisor's performance is often inhibited by the size of his or her client roster. Professional advisors, with a far smaller but more affluent client base, are able to focus on these relationships which are, as we have seen, fundamental to the success of professional advisors.

In turning to examine value inhibitors, we continue to see many substantive distinctions between the two advisor archetypes. Take, for example, product costs. Advisors are only able to moderately manage product costs on behalf of their clients because those costs are usually institutionally set. Professional advisors, in contrast, can pick and chose products from any provider.

Advisory costs (if unbundled) are of moderate-to-low importance for advisors because they are set by the institution. Professional advisors generally have higher advisory fees because of their need to be state of the art, and they also have an extensive professional support network. Similarly, relationship costs are often moderate for advisors because they are engaged in what is more of a commodity-driven business. Among professional advisors, relationship costs are high because they reflect the highly specialized services this group offers.

CREATING A PIPELINE OF ULTRA-AFFLUENT CLIENTS

The Affluent Client Value Equation^{SM} can and should permeate all aspects and ways the professional advisor does business because, when effectively employed, it can make a major difference in the way many professional advisors perform. That is because it helps them shift their thinking from the nuts-and-bolts of what they do day-in and day-out to the more esoteric world of the ultra-affluent. The Affluent Client Value Equation^{SM} proves to be particularly powerful when it comes to developing a professional advisor's business model.

Successful professional advisory practices are consciously or unconsciously constructed around the Affluent Client Value Equation^{SM}. It is the choices professional advisors make about how, where, and when they will deliver value to their ultra-affluent clients that determine their success. The Affluent Client Value Equation[SM] affects all other decisions of the practice, including organizational considerations, the business orientation, and the manner in which professional advisors choose to differentiate themselves. Put together in a seamless organization, these components will help create a pipeline of ultra-affluent clients.

In the investment advisory business, most new affluent clients come from peer (i.e., client) referrals. A comparison of referrals with the ways that professional advisors with an advance planning practice get new clients—primarily from other advisors—further underscores the differences between successful business models in these respective fields.

In advanced planning practices, relatively little business results from ultra-affluent client referrals. Instead, referrals come from the ultra-affluent client's other advisors (not necessarily professional advisors as we are defining them). This mechanism of business development affects the breadth and depth of the relationships professional advisors need to establish with both their ultra-affluent clients and other advisors who work with this important market segment.

KNOWLEDGE TRANSFER

While there are many proven and effective ways to build relationships with advisor referral sources, one of the best is knowledge transfer. Other advisors to the ultra-affluent understand that it is crucial to stay current. More importantly, they recognize that to maintain their professional relationships with their ultra-affluent clients they have to be hyper-responsive to those clients' needs and wants, which increasingly means being aware of and employing more cutting-edge solutions.

The importance of knowledge transfer is not limited to the world of the ultra-affluent. In one study, we evaluated the motivations of 106 accountants and 133 attorneys when it came to referring life insurance professionals. The empirical design of the study permitted the control of compensation for the accountants and attorneys so this issue became moot. In the case of 77.4 percent of accountants and 89.5 percent of attorneys, life insurance professionals had to be considered as a valuable business resource if they were going to be referred (Exhibit 8.4), and the best way to become a business resource was though knowledge transfer.

Exhibit 8.4

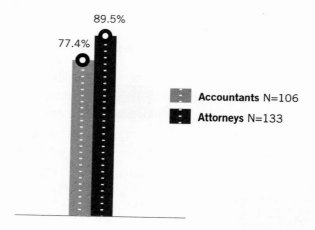

THE CASE FOR KNOWLEDGE TRANSFER

89.5%

77.4%

Accountants N=106
Attorneys N=133

These results have been replicated in more than a dozen studies conducted over the last five years, and this approach to generating new business cuts across all the professional services, including investment management, investment banking, and even strategy consulting. We consistently find that knowledge transfer is the best way for advisors — including professional advisors — to be "top-of-the-mind" with other advisors when referral opportunities arise.

CROSS-PROFESSIONAL RELATIONSHIPS

Because of the way in which new business development is done in the advanced planning field, we strongly advocate developing cross-professional relationships (Exhibit 8.5). Ideally, a professional advisor will have a number of strategic alliances with several other advisors to ultra-affluent clients. This approach results in the professional advisor having a better understanding of the business models of these other advisors, the cultivation of greater mutual trust between advisors, greater value for the ultra-affluent client, and increased revenues to all advisors involved. All of this is predicated on knowledge transfer from the professional advisor to other advisors.

Exhibit 8.5

DEVELOPING CROSS-PROFESSIONAL RELATIONSHIPS

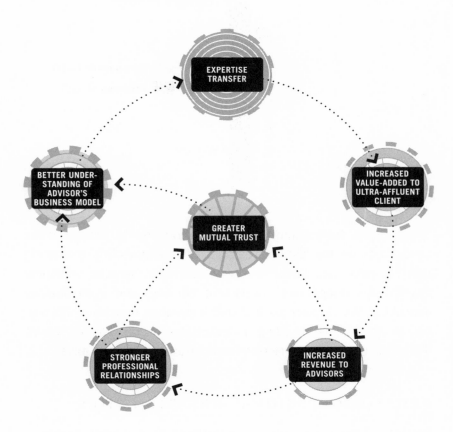

The roadblock to referrals is the common misperception among professional advisors that they need to keep their advanced planning strategies and tactics cloaked in secrecy and even erect legal barriers around their state-of-the-art ideas. They inaccurately see what is in fact ephemeral expertise as their source of sustained professional prowess. In actuality, it is the professional advisors who create relationships with other advisors based on sharing their expertise (augmented by strong interpersonal skills) who are going to be the most successful by tapping into the ultra-affluent client pipeline.

Such openness does not necessarily eliminate the need for confidentiality agreements, which can often protect and benefit professional advisors and their clients. However, based on the payback, it is essential to find the middle ground when it comes to sharing knowledge.

We need to keep in mind that for professional advisors to stay state of the art, which is integral to their effectiveness with the ultra-affluent as well as their being top-of-mind with advisor referral sources, advanced planning strategies and tactics must be constantly evolved. Professional advisors as we are defining them are always creating new knowledge, and that new knowledge translates into value for the ultra-affluent as well as for the advisors themselves.

Because information and industry trends come and go so quickly, however, it can be difficult for professional advisors to stand out in their highly competitive environment. An optimal approach is to become a technical resource for other advisors as well as the ultra-affluent. As a technical resource, other advisors who are not involved in advanced planning yet have ultra-affluent clients can better serve these clients, thereby strengthening their relationships. Freely transferring expertise to other advisors may be counterintuitive to some, but is often the best course of action for a professional advisor.

The transferring of expertise must be accomplished in context, of course. Other advisors have their own agendas and therefore will need to be worked with accordingly. Aside from generating revenue for the other advisors in their "worlds," the professional advisor must be cognizant of the working relationship he or she develops with these advisors, including the manner in which everyone is compensated. In our experience, the best professional advisors know the needs and wants of their strategic partners as surely as they know the needs and wants of their ultra-affluent clients.

Regardless of the technical proficiency of the other advisors, it is imperative that the professional advisor shares in-depth rather than superficial expertise. And, ideally, that should come through a learner-centered and constructivist approach.

For the professional advisor the role of being the go-to technical resource when it comes to advanced planning will prove to be a very advantageous business-building strategy. Besides identifying potential clients that can benefit from such expertise, the role also solidifies trust with the other advisors. Once they become a trusted resource, other advisors will come to them with concerns and questions. And all of this back-and-forth leads to higher rates of interaction, which in turn results in the professional advisor's being top-of-mind in a referral situation. Those professional advisors who attempt to restrict the transfer of expertise will be supplanted by competitors who understand and are able to manage the transfer of expertise most effectively.

SUMMARY

Since all businesses need to be differentiated, this is an essential task of a professional advisor seeking success. Ultra-affluent clients and their other advisors need to know, and be able to articulate, a reason why they go to or refer others to a particular professional advisor.

Naturally, professional advisors also want to create a pipeline of ultra-affluent clients. With a pipeline in place, they can continually upgrade their practices so that each year they manage fewer, but more profitable, clients. In this way, professional advisors can over time move from the supra-affluent to the mega-affluent and finally to the maxi-affluent. One professional advisory firm has already evolved to the point where it only caters to billionaires and generates, on average, $20 million in revenue per client every 18 months.

New analytic tools have revealed that the most effective way for professional advisors to create a pipeline of ultra-affluent clients is to win the trust and confidence of other advisors by becoming a technical resource. They also need to remain cognizant of the professional goals of their fellow advisors and be motivated to help them achieve those goals.

The analytic framework to determine how to best approach ultra-affluent clients and other advisors is embodied in the Affluent Client Value Equation^{SM}, a strategic planning algorithm that enables professional advisors to see exactly where and how much value they provide to their ultra-affluent clients and under what circumstances. In this framework, value drivers are distinguished from value inhibitors so that the clear path to delivering superior value can be discerned. Such discernment enables professional advisors to close the loop and create a pipeline of ultra-affluent clients.

THE FUTURE OF
ADVANCED PLANNING

CHANGE IS THE LAW OF LIFE. AND THOSE WHO LOOK ONLY TO THE

PAST OR THE PRESENT ARE CERTAIN TO MISS THE FUTURE.

John F. Kennedy

Anyone in the field of advanced planning realizes that it is — and will continue to be — in a state of flux. We all know that tax laws will be rewritten and regulations will be revised. We also know that assets will fluctuate as the stock market runs with the bulls and the bears over the course of time. Above all, we understand that the needs and goals of ultra-affluent clients will change. Those needs and goals will be uniquely affected by factors such as each client's age, family, and lifestyle. For the most stable of clients, relationships will be reassessed and goals reconsidered. All of that will add up to make advanced planning for the ultra-affluent a tremendous challenge for both clients and their professional advisors. It will also continue to create a highly profitable opportunity for those professional advisors who are equal to the challenge.

The main thrust of this book has been twofold: first, even though an increasing number of advisors and financial institutions are setting their sights on the ultra-affluent, professional advisors have a decided advantage. Indeed, we believe that the chief competition will continue to come from within the ranks of professional advisors, not without. Second, the most successful professional advisors will be those who can best differentiate themselves, that differentiation coming in the form of acute interpersonal skills, applicable industry knowledge and experience, and the capability to put together a network of other astute advisors to draw upon. In every aspect of their business, however, those professional advisors who are best able to anticipate and adapt to change will be the industry's leaders and its most successful practitioners, today and ten years from now.

APPENDICES

ANALYTIC MODELING

Analytic modeling is one of several methodologies used to size or estimate what cannot be measured directly, and it is the preferred approach for assessing a market such as the ultra-affluent. Because the methodology we employed is but one way of generating estimates, however, we validated its results against other modeling techniques.

At its core, analytic modeling uses a multi-equation approach to create scenarios or best-estimates of the current size of the affluent universe across predetermined, asset-sized segments. In this case, the analytic model was constructed of a series of equations, resulting in deterministic algorithms. The data the model was built on focus on a variety of issues such as the impact of tax policies on the behavior of the affluent, as well as the calculations of other analysts.

In order to create the analytic model, 27,904 data points were used. Each data point "footed" to two or more primary and/or secondary sources. These data points were obtained from 133 different sources such as think tanks, financial institutions, industry consultants, academicians, and governmental organizations. The sources included:

∴ Merrill Lynch

∴ The Spectrem Group

∴ The Global Policy Forum

∴ New York University

∴ The Lazard Trust

∴ The World Bank

∴ Cornell University

∴ The Essenes Trust

∴ FinCEN

∴ The Institute for Intergovernmental Research

∴ The Soloton Society

∴ The International Association for Research in Income and Wealth

A critical issue in the process was to ensure that we excluded any "tainted money" in the model. Thus, wherever there was a meaningful chance (i.e., a 10 percent or greater probability that the private wealth in question was a product of illegal activities as defined by the United States going back two generations) the wealth was considered to be "tainted money" and we excluded it from the model.

There are two areas to closely examine when evaluating the output of an analytic model such as this. The first is the quality of the data incorporated into the model. The old saw is "garbage in, garbage out" meaning that a model is only as good as the data upon which it is based. As noted, we address this threat to validity by closely examining each data point, requiring multiple confirmations before including it in the model. In effect, every data point was checked and double-checked, and when questions were raised and estimates were required, specific content matter experts were called in.

The other potential threat to validity is assumptions made about how core measures interact because a change in structural relationships can have a cascading effect on the calculations. We approached this issue by creating scenarios where the core measures were systematically manipulated. During this process, we conducted sensitivity analyses to provide a better understanding of the likelihood of each conclusion.

As anyone who has done modeling knows, these calculations are a function of the quality of the data introduced into the analytic model. Obviously, changes in these numbers will alter the conclusions, which is why we undertook so much model testing and paid so much attention to issues of reliability and validity.

In many places, we also needed to build in assumptions about the behaviors of the affluent. In these instances we extrapolated from the empirical studies of the high-net-worth market conducted by Prince & Associates over the last decade.

SCENARIO THINKING

Simply put, scenario thinking is multi-future thinking. Where we are uncertain of what is to come, the approach is to consider a number of possible alternatives. Scenario thinking is a critical skill for professional advisors when dealing with uncertainty and complexity, two characteristics that are at the heart of the multi-faceted advanced planning process. Requiring a high degree of intellectual openness and agility, scenario thinking is "what if" thinking that approaches decision-making as both a process and as learning. The goal of scenario thinking is to permit professional advisors to improve their "signal to noise ratio." By applying scenario thinking, they can avoid the inappropriate (but all too pervasive) reliance on heuristics such as the anchoring effect, confirmation bias, and the adjustment error. It also enables advisors to avoid the all too common and highly deleterious error of "seeing is believing."

For professional advisors, scenario thinking confers value in several ways. On one hand, it has three direct applications for advanced planners as discussed below. Scenario thinking is also valuable when it comes to developing new faculties for improved decision-making. Scenario thinking trains the mental processes of the professional advisor; those using scenario thinking become more aware of cognitive models and the forces that drive decision-makers in selected situations. This in turn facilitates the ability of the professional advisor to better work with ultra-affluent clients and their other advisors.

MANAGING UNCERTAINTY

Professional advisors regularly face high degrees of uncertainty in many aspects of their practices. Indeed, because of the changes and the pace of change that is endemic to the financial services industry, the only certainty is uncertainty.

The two principal forms of uncertainty are:

∴ Risks for which we have enough historical precedent to enable us to predict various possible outcomes. This is the world we work in and it is where scenario thinking operates.

∴ Risks that are the product of structural uncertainties and/or unknowable — the proverbial "Acts of God."

For professional advisors, scenario thinking gives them the means to find a point of reference if there is an historical precedent. Hence, they are able to develop better judgement concerning the range of probabilistic futures and to better understand the implications of various possibilities.

While we often face many uncertainties, some of the variables in the processes are indeed predictable — what we are referring to as historical precedent. These variables referred to as "predetermined elements" allow us to extrapolate and build scenarios.

In considering scenario accuracy, we need to take into account the time frame and the number of variables involved. The longer the time frame the lower the viability of any scenario (Exhibit A.1). In other words, the farther out we look, the more cloudy our vision becomes.

PREDICTABILITY AND TIME FRAME

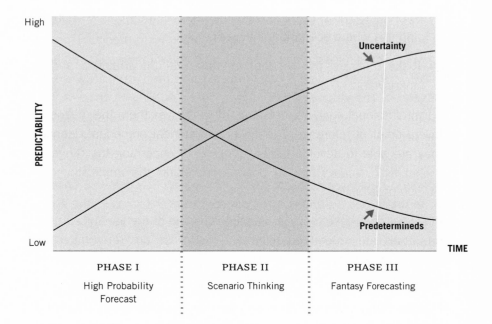

Aside from the time frame, the number of variables involved also affects our scenario creations. There is a direct relationship between the degree of uncertainty and the number of variables we focus on. Specifically, the more uncertainty, the fewer the variables we can consider. At the same time, we need to specify the extent of interaction among variables. Various sources of uncertainty must be considered orthogonally, thereby minimizing the interacting variables.

In the end, the power of scenario thinking is embedded in its ability to organize a large set of relevant but apparently discrete data points for the benefit of ultra-affluent clients and their many advisors, including professional advisors.

SCENARIO THINKING AND
ADVANCED PLANNING

In the context of advanced planning, there are three contextually specific times that scenario thinking becomes instrumental. The first is when the professional advisor is working with the ultra-affluent client. Scenario thinking is one of the steps of the Virtuous Cycle (see **Chapter 4, The Virtuous Cycle**). There are no "universal answers," so scenario thinking helps advisors consider the various ways to employ the possible range of strategies and tactics to meet the ultra-affluent client's agenda.

Scenario thinking is also part of the Innovation Process (see **Chapter 5, To the Edge**). As professional advisors work their way to the edge, they need to consider the possible outcomes and impact of their formulated strategies and tactics.

Thirdly, scenario thinking becomes important when examining advanced planning as a business (see **Chapter 8, The Advanced Planning Practice**). In the strategic management of an advanced planning practice, advisors need to always be forward looking and they need to assess the changes impacting the industry as well as their selected business model. This application of scenario thinking enables professional advisors to prepare for possible changes that can meaningfully affect their businesses.

With respect to advanced planning, we can consider the times scenario thinking is used and the appurtenance of creating meaningful scenarios (Exhibit A.2).

SCENARIO CREATION AND ADVANCED PLANNING

CREATING MEANINGFUL SCENARIOS	THE VIRTUOUS CYCLE	THE INNOVATION PROCESS	THE ADVANCED PLANNING PRACTICE
A rich variety of perspectives	Bounded by the ultra-affluent client and the current financial and legal framework	Parameters set by the current financial and legal framework as well as anticipated short-term changes	Based on industry trends and dynamics
Address critical dimensions of the situation	Focused on what can conceivably be accomplished within the preset boundaries	Often a function of the level of aggressiveness deemed acceptable	A constant process of recognizing the dual realities of both seismic and incremental changes
Appreciation for the deeper dynamic	Concentrated on the agenda of the ultra-affluent client	Concentrated on the legal and regulatory frameworks	Concentrated on the competitive and private wealth arenas

SCENARIO THINKING PRAXIS

The essential idea of scenario thinking is to work with a medium-to-longer term time frame and to consider life cycles and external events that could affect planning. In general, advanced planning should be completed on the basis of the ultra-affluent client's best estimate of his or her future. To do that, the professional advisor must be thinking about alternative futures — alternative scenarios — and anticipate how the planning would have to be altered should any of the alternative scenarios transpire. For example, many of the plans done for the ultra-affluent in the late 1990s tended to assume that the stock market valuations then in place would hold up and few people anticipated — or took into account — the recession and lower valuations that came in the wake of the bursting of the Internet bubble in 2000.

Major changes in a client's life should also be considered in scenario thinking. An ultra-affluent client may assume that he or she will remain married for the purpose of their planning, for instance, but the possibility of divorce and remarriage should always be factored in.

The same goes for advanced planning for a privately held business. Many factors can affect business valuation and operations, and therefore the plan itself. The professional advisor should take into account the general health of the client's business and the trends that would most affect that business.

SUMMARY

Scenario thinking is a way to anticipate the unexpected and all good planning must take contingencies into account. Scenario thinking looks for the significant events (internal or external to the familial unit) that are both probable and significant. In order to be explicit in scenario thinking, a factor or trend should be relatively likely to occur and also have a significant affect on the nature of the advanced plan. The three examples cited here — a bear market, a change in marital status, or reverses in a privately held business — are possible and highly significant for the ultra-affluent client's advance plan.

Professional advisors should adopt scenario thinking any time they have to deal with uncertainty and complexity in a client situation, which is almost all of the time, because it is a critical success factor for professional advisors who are working with the ultra-affluent.